PATRICK O'CONNOR, THE MURDERED MAN.

CLARK'S EDITION.

THE BERMONDSEY MURDER.

A FULL REPORT OF THE TRIAL

OF

FREDERICK GEORGE MANNING

AND

MARIA MANNING,

FOR THE

MURDER OF PATRICK O'CONNOR,

AT MINVER-PLACE, BERMONDSEY, ON THE 9TH OF AUGUST, 1849.

INCLUDING

MEMOIRS OF PATRICK O'CONNOR, FREDERICK GEORGE
MANNING, AND MARIA MANNING.

WITH THEIR PORTRAITS, AND SEVERAL OTHER ENGRAVINGS.

LONDON:
PRINTED AND PUBLISHED BY W. M. CLARK, 17, WARWICK-LANE.
1849.

JOHN SMITH & SON, BOOKSELLERS, GLASGOW.

THE BERMONDSEY MURDER.

On the south side of the Thames, in the region of tan-pits and suburban gardens known as Bermondsey, there stands a new range of small houses, known as Minver-place. Here, in one of these houses, No. 3, dwelt with his wife, for a short time antecedent to the 9th of August, a man named Frederick George Manning. Manning's father was a sergeant in the Somerset militia, and resided a long time in Taunton, where he was for many years the lessee of the market tolls, and of several turnpikes in the town and neighbourhood and other parts of Somersetshire. He also for some years kept the Bear public-house, Taunton, and was much respected in every relation of life. He died about four or five years ago, leaving his widow and Frederick George Manning, his favourite surviving son, his representatives. The father left a larger portion of his property to the subject of this sketch than to any of his other children, and a share expectant on the death of the mother, which shortly afterwards occurred.

Manning's first connexion with his wife is involved in some obscurity. He was formerly in the service of the Great Western Railway Company, as guard, and there is no doubt was implicated in the extensive robberies which were committed on that line. It will be recollected, that, in the short space of a twelvemonth, bullion, in boxes, to the amount of £4000, was stolen from the train of which Manning was guard. He was discharged from the company's service, and was not again heard of until the mail robbery took place, in January last; and, as no clue could be found to the plunder from the up-mail, suspicion immediately alighted upon Manning and his wife. Here it should be observed, that Manning had some months before become landlord of the White Hart Inn, at Taunton, where for the first time Mrs. Manning appeared. They were both taken into custody, and after undergoing an examination were dismissed, in consequence of no property being found in their possession, at the same time it was quite clear that the prisoners were connected with the robbery, and participated in the plunder. In fact, Nightingale, Poole's confederate, whilst staying at Exeter, assumed the name of Manning.

The rumours circulated at Taunton with respect to the Mannings' connexion with Poole and Nightingale (who were subsequently convicted before Lord Denman, at the spring assizes at Exeter, and sentenced to fifteen years' transportation), proved so detrimental to the White Hart, and they were looked upon with such suspicion, that it was found necessary to

NO. 3, MINVER-PLACE, THE SCENE OF THE MURDER.

dispose of the business, Manning and his wife leaving Taunton and coming up to London, where, in a few weeks, they opened a beer-shop in the vicinity of the Hackney-road; but this lasted a very short time, and the place was abruptly closed up by Mrs. Manning absconding, taking with her the greater part of the property. This was done at the wish of the deceased, Patrick O'Connor, who had prepared a home for Mrs. Manning at another part of the metropolis. Manning traced her, through the cabman who had driven her to O'Connor's house. They made up matters, and remained for some time in apartments, and eventually took possession of the house where the murder was afterwards committed.

Maria Manning's maiden name was De Roux. She is a native of Lausanne, in Switzerland, and inherited some small patrimony from her parents, both of whom are deceased. About six years since she served in the family of Sir Lawrence Palk, at Haldon House, Devonshire, as maid to Lady Palk; and while travelling to and fro with this family it is supposed she made the acquaintance of Manning, who was at that time a guard on the Great Western Railway. At the decease of Lady Palk, in the year 1846, she obtained a situation as maid to Lady Blantyre, the second daughter of the Duchess of Sutherland. She came to reside with her ladyship at Stafford House, in July, 1846, and accompanied her to Scotland in the autumn of the same year. While attending her ladyship on a brief continental tour, before proceeding to Scotland, she met with the deceased, O'Connor, who seems to have been struck with her appearance and manners—so much so as to have offered her marriage. In the early part of the season 1847 she returned to town with Lady Blantyre, and it appears was frequently visited at Stafford House by both Manning and O'Connor, the latter of whom appeared to entertain a very warm affection for her. Manning, however, seems to have been the most favoured suitor, and on the 27th of May, 1847, she was married to him at St. James's Church, Piccadilly. After her marriage she accompanied Manning into Devonshire for a week or ten days; and then, returning to Stafford House, went with Lady Blantyre to the Continent a second time, one motive for her doing so being, as it is alleged, the opportunity it afforded of arranging her own affairs abroad previously to settling down to married life in England.

On her return from the Continent she went to reside with her husband in lodgings at 2, Church-street, Paddington, Manning still filling the situation of guard on the Great Western Railway. We should here state, that it is believed, Manning, in prosecuting his addresses, succeeded in persuading Maria De Roux that he was entitled to property under his mother's will, amounting to between £600 and £700. This was of course only a fiction; but so deeply did he lay his schemes that he actually drew up a will, which has been found among the papers in his wife's possession, by which he bequeathed this property to his "very dear and beloved wife," to the exclusion of all other claimants, appointing her executor, conjointly with Henry Poole, recently convicted of the mail robberies on the Great Western Railway, who is one of the subscribing witnesses to the deed. There does not appear to be the least reason to believe that Manning had any property himself, but with the money he obtained from his wife, very shortly after their marriage, he took the public-house at Taunton.

Patrick O'Connor, the wretched victim, first arrived in London from Ireland in February, 1832, or at least early in the spring of that year. He had a letter of introduction from his brother, now priest of the rich parish of Templemore, near Thurles, county of Tipperary, to a gentleman of influence, living at the time in chambers in the Temple. The gentleman in question is a native of Ireland, and a friend of the murdered man's brother, the Reverend Father O'Connor. The gentleman received O'Connor kindly for his reverend brother's sake, and asked him what were his views, and the nature of the situation he was seeking for. O'Connor said he wished to enter the police, and the gentleman, to forward his views, gave him a letter to Mr. Mayne, one of the police commissioners. It is probable the letter was never delivered by O'Connor, for a few days after he had received it he changed his mind and said he would not become "a thief taker."

In about six weeks after his first introduction he called on the gentleman, and, much to the latter's surprise, he produced a £50 note, and requested the gentleman to take care of it for him. The gentleman took charge of the note, and knowing O'Connor's poverty, eagerly enquired how he became possessed of it. The latter said his mother had sent him £15, with which he had purchased contraband tobacco and cigars, and trading surreptitiously in them, had amassed the amount of the £50 note. The gentleman at the time believed the story to be true, and as O'Connor was then endeavouring to obtain a situation in the Excise, he told him ironically that his practical knowledge of smuggling would, no doubt, if known to the Excise commissioners, prove a great recommendation in his favour. Before the close of the year 1832, Patrick O'Connor had placed in the gentleman's hands no less altogether than £184, £100 of which the gentleman invested in the funds at O'Connor's request. This rapid accumulation of money excited the gentleman's surprise, and almost his suspicions that everything was not right. In the winter 1832-33 O'Connor obtained, through the influence of the late Bishop of Llandaff, we believe, the situation of tide-waiter in the port of London. In the meantime he had been, bit by bit, withdrawing from the gentleman's hands the £84 not invested; and got back the last of it to buy a bed, which he said he was obliged to take about with him from one ship to another in the Thames, in the discharge of his new duties. He had hardly been installed in the situation of tide-waiter, when he sent his attorney's letter to the gentleman demanding payment of the whole sum of £184. The gentleman p-had no acknowledgement from O'Connor that he had received back £84 of it; and probably legal proceedings would have been instituted, had not the gentleman, through his solicitor, who was a friend of the solicitor of O'Connor, proved the latter's dishonesty by means of the gentleman's laundress, to whom O'Connor, on discovering that she was a widow, with a pension of £26 a year, and earning in the Temple, as laundress to several legal gentlemen, nearly £100 a year besides, made a proposal of marriage, and showed her one evening fifty pounds, which he said he had just received from her master, being, a portion of money lent to him. O'Connor's solicitor, on hearing this, refused to have anything more to do with him, and the gentleman sold out stock to the amount of £100, and through his solicitor returned O'Connor his money. The woman in question was a respectable Irishwoman, living rent free in the kitchens attached to the gentleman's chambers, receiving £15 a year from him for her services, and it is more than probable she would have married O'Connor had she not discovered his ingratitude and want of probity.

After this transaction the gentleman made inquiries as to O'Connor's method of raising money, and he found that he had got introduced to the late Bishop of Llandaff, Mr. Darby, M.P., and other proselyting Protestants, and that he knew of the Bexley fund, appropriated to the conversion of Roman Catholics, chiefly to the religion of the Established Church. To these gentlemen O'Connor represented himself as one persecuted for his religious doubts by his brother, the Rev. Dr. O'Connor, and other Catholic clergymen; and he also alleged, there not being the slightest ground for the truth of the allegation, that his brother had wronged him respecting money bequeathed to the family by the Misses Tobin, who had been nuns in the ancient Ursuline convent of Thurles. By these representations O'Connor insinuated himself into the good graces of the Bishop of Llandaff, Mr. Darby, Mr. Broderick, the grandson of the then Archbishop of Cashel, the late Lady Osborne, mother of Mr. Bernal Osborne, the member for Middlesex, and others, and obtained from them not only large sums of money, but the situation that afterwards led to his connexion with the Customs as a gauger in the London Docks. Promotion to the latter situation is understood to be owing to the influence of Mr Sheil, when one of the commissioners of Greenwich Hospital, who was indebted for his election to represent Tipperary chiefly to the exertions of Dr. O'Connor, Father Laffan, Mr. P. Fogarty, and other friends of O'Connor. Patrick O'Connor appears to have been a man who would do anything for money; and it is more than probable, that a passion for the person of Mrs. Manning was not the main cause of his intimacy with her and her husband, but rather that it was based on his being leagued with Manning in some money-getting transactions and speculations.

The circumstances under which O'Connor made the acquaintance of Maria de Roux are as follow:—

In the early part of the year 1846, O'Connor, having obtained a fortnight's leave of absence, took it into his head to go to Boulogne. He embarked at London-Bridge wharf, on board one of the London and Boulogne boats, in which Maria de Roux was also a passenger, she being then on her way to join Lady Blantyre, on the Continent. In the evening, after all the other passengers had retired to bed, O'Connor and Maria de Roux were left together in the saloon cabin, and here their first intimacy commenced. She appears to have communicated her name and the position she occupied to O'Connor without any reserve, for upon his return to England he mentioned the fact of having met such a lady to his friends, and expressed his intention of calling upon her at Stafford House as soon as she returned from the Continent. That he did so, and that a correspondence was kept up between the two parties for some time, is also known, O'Connor having frequently spoken of visits he had made to Stafford House, and also exhibited letters received from Maria de Roux. One of these letters indicated that she was expecting or desiring that O'Connor should make her his wife; for she asks him, "Of what good is it to continue our correspondence? You never speak of marriage." Among his friends the deceased made no secret of his intimacy with Maria de Roux, but he never led any of them to believe that he had any serious intention of marrying her. His object seemed rather to be, to make it appear that he had great influence over her, and that she was very fond of him. On one occasion in company where O'Connor was, the conversation turned upon the favourite actress, Madame Celeste, and a person present remarked on the very engaging effect which her peculiar accentuation had upon the audience. O'Connor remarked that he greatly admired it himself, and that her pronunciation of the English language was very like that of "Mauridhe Rhua," as he was accustomed to style Maria de Roux. Following up the observation, he remarked that she wrote as she spoke, and, producing a note, he handed it to a friend present, and requested her to read it aloud. After perusing a few lines, the lady saw that it was, in common parlance, a "love letter;" and on making a remark to that effect, O'Connor laughed, and appeared highly delighted that his ascendancy over Maria de Roux should be generally known. When de Roux married Manning, it is quite true that O'Connor addressed a letter to her, upbraiding her with infidelity to him; but his friends believe that this was sheer hypocrisy, and that he cared nothing whatever about the matter. "Mauridhe Rhua," the name by which O'Connor always designated Mrs. Manning, is a Hibernian expression, signifying "Red Mary."

The following are copies of notes written by Mrs. Manning to Patrick O'Connor, on the two Wednesdays preceding the murder. They both bear the Borough post-mark, and are stamped as delivered respectively on the 1st and 8th August, as directed. The letters are copied verbatim at discretion: it will be seen that the first especially betrays the writer's imperfect knowledge of the English language. It runs thus:—

"Dear O'Connor: I shall be most happy to see you this day to my House to dinner at ½ o'clock. Yours affection, MARIA MANNING.—P. O'Connor, Guager, London Dock.—(Wild)—Wednesday morning."

It is not known whether the deceased dined with the Mannings on this day; but on the following Wednesday he received the annexed note:—

"Dear O'Connor: We shall be happy to see you to dine with us to-day, at half-past 5 o'clock. Yours affection, MARIA MANNING.—P. O'Connor, Guager, London Dock.—Wednesday morning."

This note invited the deceased to dinner on the day preceding his murder. He did not dine in Minver-place on this day; but, accompanied by Mr. Walshe, went there at a late hour in the evening, and left after having had his temples rubbed by Mrs. Manning with eau de Cologne, in consequence of his feeling rather faint. The Mannings did not ask O'Connor to dine with them on the following day in the presence of Mr. Walshe; they were apparently too artful for that, and delayed inviting him until the following morning, when Mrs. Manning again wrote to him, at the London Docks, a note which the unhappy man is proved to have shown his friends Messrs. Keating and Graham, on meeting them on London Bridge, as he was on his way to be murdered. This note was of course destroyed by his assassins, as nothing has been seen of it since.

Patrick O'Connor was last seen alive on the night of Thursday, the 9th of August; as late as ten o'clock, smoking and in conversation with Mrs. Manning. On the morning of Friday the deceased was absent from his duty at the London Docks, and the day wore on without his coming. It was the same on Saturday. Sunday and Monday lapsed, and no tidings of him reached his friends; and on Tuesday sinister apprehensions began to be entertained respecting his fate. An acquaintance who had spoken to him on London Bridge on the evening of Thursday, came forward and stated that he had told him he was on his way to Manning's house at Bermondsey; and as his intimacy with this family was well known, inquiries were instituted there by his surviving relatives and the police, who had been apprised of his suspicious absence. These inquiries were answered by Mrs. Manning with coolness and composure, and conjecture was therefore completely at fault as to what had become of the missing man.

Two days later, that is to say, on the 17th of August, the police, in the prosecution of their researches, returned to the house. "The nest was there, but the birds had fled." Manning and his wife had left in "hot haste," stripping the house of all its furniture, which was afterwards discovered to have been sold "in a lump" to a neighbouring broker. Strengthened by this circumstance in their suspicions, the police effected an entry upon the premises, and explored the apartments and garden. Even this was in vain, until one of the officers, more sharp-sighted or better-informed on the subject than the others, thought he detected some trace of recent removal in one of the flagstones with which the back kitchen was paved, and trying the mortar of the joints with his knife, found it to be quite soft. Upon this they proceeded to take up the flags and remove the earth beneath; when, in a square oblong hole filled up with quicklime, they discovered the body of O'Connor, lying on its face, and with its legs trussed up to the haunches, to make it fit the receptacle. So rapidly had the lime done its work in consuming the corpse, that its identity was only established by the remarkable and less perishable features of an extremely prominent chin and a set of false teeth. This was on the Friday. On the Wednesday preceding, Mrs. Manning had been interrogated upon that very spot on the subject of O'Connor's absence; and it is presumed the murder took place on the night of the Thursday preceding—that is to say, five clear days before. Yet all this while, as she had no servant, she must have performed the ordinary occupations of a household in this kitchen—a fact inferentially proved by the statement of one of the witnesses—that the room was very clean on the day the police called for the first time to make inquiries after the murdered man; and she must have cooked the food she ate, and perhaps consumed the clothes he wore, at the fire which was so close to the body of the victim as almost to be capable of imparting warmth to his corpse.

The house which has been the scene of such a dreadful tragedy, and of which we give the ground-plan on the opposite page, is one of a newly-built and apparently respectably tenanted row, consisting of six rooms—two kitchens on the basement, with parlours, and a floor above them, and is approached from the street by a flight of several stone steps. It was taken by the supposed murderers at Midsummer last.

How Patrick O'Connor was murdered is not known, further than the fact that he had seventeen wounds on the back of his head, and a pistol bullet lodged in the skin over the right eye. It is possible that he was slain in a state of intoxication. That he was an abstemious man in the matter of strong drink, is admitted by all his friends; but it is also stated that he was latterly in mortal fear of cholera, and that he had been seen drunk with brandy or port wine, which he had taken as a preventive of that disease. That he may have been induced to partake of strong liquors, under the fear of cholera, is by no means

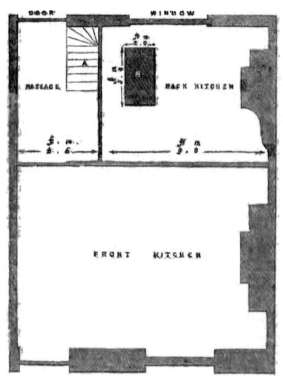

GROUND-PLAN OF MANNING'S HOUSE, SHOWING THE HOLE WHERE
THE BODY WAS FOUND.

an improbable supposition, though the idea that stupefaction was caused by steeping his tobacco in laudanum is much more probable, seeing that the *post mortem* examination did not indicate the presence of opium in the stomach by the smell; but, at all events, it is nearly certain that he was insensible when he was murdered, that he was in a recumbent position, very likely lying a-bed, and that he lay on his left side, with his face rather downwards. All the wounds on his head—which were sufficient to cause death, without going beyond them to look for another cause—were at the right side; and the bullet, which may have been fired at him to finish the work begun with the blunt cutting instrument wherewith these fractures were effected, was found over the right eye, as if driven through the head from the rear. That this was the case, and that the projectile in question was propelled by an insufficient power, is obvious from the fact that the bullet lodged in the skin over the right eye. This would lead in some sort to the conclusion that it was fired from a badly-loaded air-gun, or with a small charge of gun-cotton from a common pistol or other fire-arm. The course of this wound, however, shows that it was not fatal; and, therefore, the murder must have been consummated with a heavy hammer or some similar instrument, for the back part of the skull was found entirely beaten in fragments into the brain by the violence of successive blows.

From circumstances that have since transpired, very little doubt exists that the murder of O'Connor was premeditated for some time, and that the house in Minver-place was actually taken for that purpose. The Mannings, through their extravagance and dissipation, had got rid of nearly all their property, with the exception of the furniture, and their circumstances became critical; scarcely had they been a week in the house than suspicion was excited amongst the inhabitants of the neighbourhood by their extraordinary conduct. They appeared, to use the words of the person who resides next door, "to be up all night; there was nearly always a light burning; and there always appeared to be something mysterious going on."—Mr. O'Connor, the deceased, was frequently at the house, and his jocularity with Mrs. Manning was markedly observed by the persons residing in the houses on either side. He was almost always to be seen smoking, in the company of Manning, at the back-parlour window, and also in the small garden at the rear of the house. That a *liaison* had for some time existed between the deceased and Mrs. Manning, is quite certain; and that Manning was aware of the fact is equally apparent, for as late as Thursday, the 9th of August, the day on which he was supposed to have been murdered, Manning and O'Connor were in the garden smoking together. The deceased seems to have been frequently cautioned by his friends to discontinue his visits to Mrs. Manning; but he always observed in reply, that he did not fear any harm, as they were on the best terms, and he did not like to abandon an old companion. In order to show that the act was long premeditated, as far back as the 11th of July Manning went to the shop of Mr. Evans, ironmonger, in King William-steeet, City, to purchase a crow-bar, about 11lb. weight, for, as he said, to lift heavy things up, "such as stones." It is pretty clear, from the appearance of the place where the body was concealed, that it had been some time before prepared, and an instrument of the kind would be necessary to raise up the stones, which are large Yorkshire flags.

INQUEST ON THE BODY.

The inquisition was taken, August 18, at the New Leather-market Tavern, New Westen street, Bermondsey, by Mr. Carter, one of the Coroners for Surrey, and a jury of thirteen of the most respectable tradesmen in the neighbourhood. Fourteen jurymen had been sworn, but Mr. J. Meade, a friend of deceased's, objected to one of them, viz. Mr. Coleman, builder and owner of the house in which the murdered body was found, on the ground that he would be required as a witness. The Coroner allowed the objection, and the name of Mr. Coleman was struck off the jury-list.

The jury having been sworn,

The Coroner said: Gentlemen, the first thing I shall have to call upon you to do is, to see the body, and then I shall call witnesses to identify it. When the body is identified I can give an order for interment, to be carried into effect, of course, only after the body has been examined by the medical gentleman that may be appointed to do so by this Court.

The jury then went and took a view of the body. It was still naked as it was found, the legs and thighs having been tied up to the body with a new rope. Though but partially covered with lime, decomposition had rapidly set in, or, at any rate, there was extensive discolouration of the face, neck, and thorax; and it was only by the chin (deceased had a remarkably thin and projecting one), and a set of false teeth, that those best acquainted with deceased could identify the body.

The first witness called and sworn was

Mr. Pierce Walshe, who said: I have seen the body of a man at No. 3, Minver-place, New Weston-street, in the parish of Bermondsey, and I have not the slightest reasonable doubt as to the identity of that body. I recognise it by its features; and the person to whom it belonged was named Patrick O'Connor, who was a ganger in the London Docks. I think his

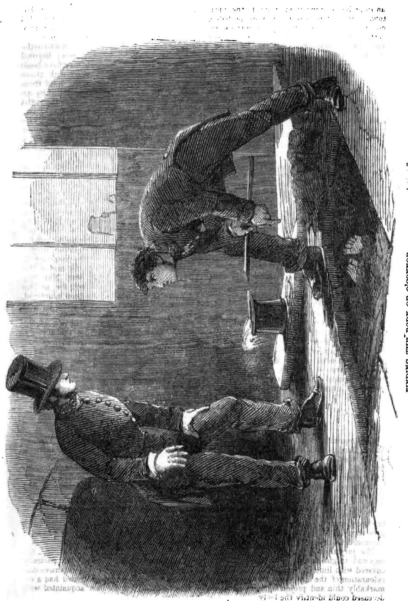

FINDING THE BODY OF O'CONNOR.

The first witness called and sworn was...

Mr. Pierce Walshe, who said : I have seen the body of the man at Mr. Glover-place, Weston-street, in the parish of Bermondsey, and I have not the least reasonable doubt to the identity of that body. I recognise it by its features as the person to whom it belonged was named Patrick O'Connor, who was a person ... ... Custom House Docks. I think I...

age was about fifty. I have known him personally since the 26th of April last. He was my personal friend, and his sister is married to a cousin of mine. He resided at 21, Greenwood-street, Mile-end, and was a single man. I was with him at No. 8, Minver-place, on Wednesday, the 8th of August, and saw him last alive at twelve o'clock that night. We parted at the corner of Commercial-street, Whitechapel, after having been at No. 8, Minver-place. He was then in a good state of health.

The inquest was then adjourned.

The adjourned inquest was resumed on the 24th, when, among several other witnesses, the following were examined:—

Henry Barnes, police constable 256, K division, proceeded on Friday the 17th, in company with police-constable Burton, of the M division, to No. 8, Minver-place, New Weston-street, Bermondsey. On arriving there, Burton unlocked the door of the house and went in. Burton had the key in his possession. There was no other person in our company. We looked in the front and back parlour, and then in the front kitchen. We then went into the back kitchen—it was on a level with the front under ground. The back kitchen was flagged over with large flag stones; all the rooms were quite empty. I observed a damp mark along the edges of two of the stones, which induced us to take out our knives and try the mortar. I found it was wet. Burton did the same. I then told Burton I should not be satisfied until those two stones were taken up; and Burton went out and borrowed a shovel, a crowbar, and a boat-hook without a handle. We then prised up the smallest of the two stones; and I remarked to Burton that the stone was never laid by a mason, because it had mortar all under it: it had a bed of mortar under it, instead of the mortar being merely round the edges. We then removed the other stones, which had the same appearance. I took the shovel and removed the mortar and earth, assisted by Burton, who used the crowbar. At about the depth of twelve inches, I found a piece of linen rag. It was about the size of both my hands, and I took it up and smelt it. I remarked to Burton that it smelt very much as if it had belonged to a dead body, and if we proceeded we should most likely find the body. We then continued the digging, when I saw something else which I thought was another white rag. I took hold of it and shook it, and said, "Here is the toe of a man." Burton was then about to leave for assistance, but I said "Wait a moment," and I removed the earth and exposed the whole foot. Burton then went to the station for some assistance, which came, and I dug on further until I came to the person's loins, and, with assistance, we found the dead body of a man there, lying on his face. The body was buried in unslacked lime, with the legs tied up round the haunches with stout cord: they were bent back. Before the body was removed from the hole, Mr. Lockwood (the surgeon) came, and I saw him take from the mouth a set of false teeth, which he washed in water, which we had at hand. The body was then taken out and removed into the front kitchen: it was quite naked. I should think it had been dead a fortnight, by the smell. The body was buried in a casing of lime two inches thick, and there was about eighteen inches of earth above that. A Mr. Flynn was brought from the City, and he identified the body as being that of Mr. Patrick O'Connor. On the morning of this day week, previous to finding the body, I went to 21, Greenwood-street, Mile End-road, and was shown a box, which was said to be Mr. O'Connor's. The box was locked when we examined it on the previous Monday. We then sealed it up, and we found it sealed on the Friday morning. It was opened on the Monday by Mr. Flynn. He forced it open. There was a cash box on the top of some papers, which was unlocked. We opened it, and there were three compartments in it, but there was nothing in them. There were a quantity of memoranda, I O U's, and other papers, under one of the compartments. On Friday the box was thoroughly searched, but nothing of consequence was found. A basket, full of letters, was found, and among them some of old dates from Mrs. Manning, but none of recent date.

James Burton, 272 M: On Tuesday night, the 14th inst., about half-past eight o'clock, in consequence of three friends of the deceased Mr. O'Connor coming to the police station, where I was on duty, to make inquiries respecting the deceased, Mr. Inspector Cowland directed me to make inquiries as to what became of him. I proceeded with Mr. Meade and the other two gentlemen to No. 3, Minver-place, New Weston-street, and finding the house closed up, I went through the adjoining house, and got over the back wall, with the intention of examining the premises. During the time I was getting over the wall, Mr. Meade got the key of the house, and opened the front door. I then, in company with Mr. Meade and the two other gentlemen, looked over the house. By the appearance I thought the house had been left in a very confused state. In the front kitchen there was a quantity of linen. In the back kitchen, over the two stones where the deceased was subsequently found, a large box or portmanteau was lying open. In and around the box there was a quantity of female wearing apparel; also a railway guard's coat: these things about covered the two stones. In each of the other rooms there were things strewed about. I looked over all the things which I found, but I found nothing which Mr. Meade and his friends supposed to belong to Mr. O'Connor. At that time we had no suspicion that the body was there. Next morning a Mr. Bainbridge came and tried to unlock the door, but he did not succeed, as we had put the latch-key, in the previous night. Mr. Bainbridge then went to the station-house, and I followed him, and at the station he wished to know the reason why we had gone to the house the previous night, and I heard him say that he had purchased the goods from Manning for £13, but that he had not taken the railway coat and some other things away: the linen he said he had nothing to do with. He gave his name at the station, and said that Manning had just left his house. We then returned to the house and stopped there, and saw him take away the remainder of the goods, with the exception of the linen. Amongst the things which he took away was a shovel, which stood against the copper-hole—that was in the back kitchen. I handed that to Mr. Bainbridge myself. On the Friday I went to the house about twelve o'clock in the day-time, accompanied by Barnes, to make a full search. We went down into the back kitchen. I was standing on the nearest stone to the window, and I said to Barnes, "Here are two stones which look fresh," and Barnes took his knife out of his pocket, and tried the sides of the two stones. He found the mortar soft, and it smelt sour, like fresh mortar. Barnes tried the joints of other stones, and found the mortar hard enough. We then proposed to take the stones with the soft mortar up. We received no information which caused us to do this. We removed two of the stones, which were together about five feet long and two feet wide. On removing them, Barnes drew my attention to the untradesmanlike way in which the stones had been laid, because there was mortar in the middle. On removing the mortar we found a very hard substance, and the earth appeared to have been trodden down. I eased the earth with the crow-bar, and Barnes shovelled it out. We proceeded a little way, when Barnes pulled out a piece of rag, and after proceeding a little further, Barnes drew my attention to the toe of the deceased. He then removed the remainder of the earth and exposed a portion of the foot of a person. The body could not have sustained any injury from the crow-bar. I then went and procured further assistance, and when I returned with Mr. Yates from the station, and Mr. Burton, both inspectors, I saw a portion of the flesh, but I could not say whether it was the back or loins. I then, by direction of Mr. Yates, went for the friends of a gentleman of the name of O'Connor, who was missing, of whom inquiries had been previously made. I procured the assistance of Mr. Flynn and Mr. O'Connor, the brother of the deceased, who returned with me. Upon my return the body was in the front kitchen—it was the body of a man. The body was covered with lime. I should think it was four feet deep where the head was lying. The body must have been there for some time. We found in the back bedroom a black satin stock, but it cannot be identified as belonging to the deceased. I found no stain of blood upon it. We examined the rooms most minutely, but there were no stains of blood. There were marks on the ceiling of the back room, but I do not think they were caused by any act of violence. Think they might have been occasioned by the removal of a bedstead. We discovered no weapon of any kind about the house. We had not been engaged in excavation more than ten minutes when we discovered the deceased's toe. No person had intimated to us a knowledge of where the deceased was.

Samuel Lockwood, surgeon, deposed: Am not at present practising my profession. I was in the neighbourhood of New Weston-street on Friday last, and some information I then received caused me to go to No. 3, Minver-place, about half-past one o'clock P.M. I saw two policemen at the door, and on my announcing myself as a surgeon, they admitted me. I went down steps into the back kitchen, and there found that the slabs had been removed; and that digging was going on. I saw the feet of a person exposed in a hole, the body being yet buried in the earth. The earth was then removed, and I noticed that the legs were bent backwards against the haunches, and firmly tied there, which gave rise to the exposure of the toe. The head was considerably lower buried than the feet. I assisted in removing the dirt very carefully, being afraid that some injury might be done to the head of the body by the shovel. When we got to the head, I found a very extensive fracture on the superior part of the head, rather behind. It was large enough for me to introduce my two fingers into it. I had seen the placards stating that a person was missing, who wore a set of false teeth; and the circumstance being alluded to at this time, I removed the dirt from the head and face partially, to feel if there were any teeth in the mouth. I found a full set of false teeth in the person's mouth, and I delivered them up to Mr. Slow, the summoning officer, after washing them. The body was raised shortly afterwards in my presence, and carried into the front kitchen. I noticed a considerable quantity of lime round about the body attached to it. The body was blue and in a state of decomposition. On examining the body after it was raised, and in the presence of Mr. Odling, I found another fracture at the back of the head, on the right side. Mr. Odling also called my attention to a prominence—a small hard lump— over the right eye-brow. There was no external wound; and on my cutting down upon the prominence, I extracted from it a rather large leaden slug or bullet, weighing nearly three drachms. No weapon that might have discharged such a bullet was found on the premises to my knowledge.

Mr. George Odling was called and examined by the Coroner: I reside at No. 159, High-street, Borough, and am divisional surgeon to the M division of Metropolitan Police. I was sent for about three o'clock on Friday last, by the police, to proceed to No. 3, Minver-place. There I saw the dead body of a man, lying on his face, with his legs tied back in a hole in the back kitchen. The legs were in a reflex position, and the body was covered with lime— that is to say, the surface of the body had lime adhering to it. I examined the body in part as it lay, and I discovered that the head was fractured. The body was eventually removed into the front kitchen, where I made a further examination, and discovered a foreign body or substance under the integuments over the right eye. That substance was lodged and I could move it. I pointed it out to Mr. Lockwood, who has been examined to-day, and he with a lancet then extracted the substance, which turned out to be a leaden bullet. At that time I did not make any further examination of the head; and beyond the fracture and the bullet I did not discover any other injury to the body likely to have caused death. I have since made a *post mortem* examination, assisted by Mr. Lockwood. Before doing so we examined the body externally, and found no other injuries except those which I have already mentioned. I opened the head and abdomen, but not the chest, because I did not think it necessary, as there was no wound externally, and the other injuries, which were apparent, were sufficient to have destroyed life. The head was first opened. I removed the greater portion of the hair, and, having done so, examined the head externally. The scalp exhibited as many as eighteen wounds, many severe and deep—some deeper than others. They were, on the right side, on the top, and at the back of the head. These appeared to have been, for the most part, but not all, inflicted by a blunt instrument, for the bone was not cut, as would have been the case if it had been a sharp instrument. They might have been produced by the back or sharp part of a hammer, about an inch and a half wide, such as a bricklayer's hammer, without a division. Finding so many injuries to the scalp, I reflected it, and, of course, thereby exposed the bone, and found the cranium fractured and separated into many pieces, some of which I now produce to the jury. They are sixteen in number, and formed part of the cranium of the deceased. There were many more pieces uncollected, which I might have taken, with fissures or cracks.

The Coroner: Can you, in consequence of the cranium being destroyed in the manner you have described, account for the fact of the bullet being found between the cranium and the scalp?—Witness: No. The injuries to the cranium and scalp clearly could not have been done by the bullet. There was, however, an internal opening within about half an inch from the precise spot where the bullet was found lodged.

The Coroner: Can you form any conclusion as to how the bullet came in the position in which you found it?—Witness: It is impossible to say, but I should think it came from some of the fractures which were apparent at the back of the head.

The Coroner: And in consequence of those extensive fractures you could not detect where the bullet had entered?—Witness: No, I could not. There was one part of the surface which had a dark appearance, such as gunpowder would make.

Mr. William Massey was next sworn. He said: I am a medical student, and reside at Swarkestone, a village in Derbyshire. I formerly lodged at No. 3, Minver-place. I left there a month ago last Saturday. I had lodged there nine or ten weeks previously. Frederick George Manning and Maria his wife were my landlord and landlady. There was no other member of the family. Maria's Manning's maiden name was Maria de Roux. I ascertained this from seeing marks on certain linen articles in my rooms. I took my meals with Mr. and Mrs. Manning frequently while I lived there. They kept no domestic servant, but engaged a person occasionally to clean the rooms. I have seen Mr. O'Connor there. I was introduced to him by Manning. During the time I lodged there, I think Mr. O'Connor dined three times with Mr. and Mrs. Manning. He appeared to be on friendly terms with them. I visited Mr. O'Connor at his own lodgings twice in company with Mr. and Mrs. Manning. I never observed any improper degree of familiarity between Mr. O'Connor and Mrs. Manning. I should say they appeared very friendly together, but I had no idea there was anything wrong going on between them.

Coroner: Did you ever hear the Mannings speak of the circumstances of the deceased man?—Witness: Yes, frequently. I have heard both of them speak of him as a man of property—as being worth £20,000.

Coroner: Have you ever had any conversation with Mr. Manning in reference to the deceased O'Connor?—Witness: Yes; I have conversed with Manning, and also with his wife, in reference to Mr. O'Connor.

Coroner: Tell the Court what passed.—Witness: Well, one night about eight o'clock, when I came home to Minver-place, I found Manning sitting in my room. I sat down with him, and had a pipe and some half-and-half, and in the course of conversation he asked me what drug would be most likely to produce stupefaction, or partial intoxication, so as to "cause a person to put his hand to paper." He said his wife had been to the Docks and seen Mr. O'Connor in a state of intoxication, and that he had taken her home to his lodgings and shown her his will, in which he had made over all, or a considerable portion of his property to her. Mrs. Manning was in my room when he said this. Previous to this conversation about the will, Manning asked me—I believe I had been reading a medical work—which part of the skull was the most dangerous to injure.

A Juror: Did you inform him?—Witness: Yes; I think I told him that behind the ear was the most vulnerable point. Upon another occasion our conversation turned upon Rush, and he asked me whether I thought a murderer went to heaven. I replied "No," and quoted a text of Scripture to that effect. Manning proposed getting O'Connor to his house, and said to me and his wife, "Frighten him well," when he comes, about the cholera, and persuade him to take much brandy." This was on the same occasion as when the will was mentioned.

Coroner: Did he ask you to bring him to the house?—The witness: Mr. O'Connor had been very kind to me and my brother at the Docks, and I certainly had invited him myself to come and dine with us at Manning's, but I believed Manning to have addressed the remark, "Send him (O'Connor) to come here," to his own wife, and to have intended the other part, "and persuade him to drink large quantities of brandy when he comes, and frighten him well about the cholera," for me as well as for his wife, perhaps. He hinted about putting some stupifying drink into the brandy.

Coroner: Did you ever see any weapons in the house?—Witness: No; but I recollect Manning asking me this question, "Have you ever had, or fired off, an air-gun;" and what sort of a weapon it was? I said I had not had one, but I had seen one fired off in some experiments on natural philosophy that I had attended. He asked me if it made any noise. I told him I thought not; but it was some years since I had seen the experiment.

A Juror: Did he ever ask you to procure him any drugs?—Witness: Never.

Coroner: You said he asked you what were the most stupifying drugs?—Witness: Yes. He once asked me whether chloroform and landanum were not used as stupifying draughts, and I told him that they were. I had no apprehension of his having any design in speaking of this. On one occasion he said to me, "For God's sake, never marry a foreigner; for if you do, she will be the ruin of you." Some time before I left him he wanted to get me out of his house; and so did his wife also. I asked him for my bill, and they would hardly ever give it me. It was sent home to my parents with an overcharge, and I told them not to pay it. I afterwards obtained a proper bill, with a reduction. I left town a fortnight ago last Monday, and for eight days before that I had been living at Mr. Bainbridge's, the broker.

Other witnesses having proved the purchase of some lime, and also of a shovel, the inquest was again adjourned; and after a lengthened investigation, on the 26th of August, the jury returned a verdict, "That the deceased was Patrick O'Connor, and that he had been wilfully murdered by Frederick George Manning and Maria his wife."

PURSUIT AND CAPTURE OF THE MURDERERS.

It having been suspected that the Mannings were endeavouring to leave England in the Victoria, a vessel bound for New York, application was made to the authorities of the dockyard at Portsmouth, and Admiral Capel forthwith ordered the Fire Queen, Government steamer, to get up her steam and proceed in chase of the Victoria. The vessel left Gosport at half-past eight P.M., and continued stern chase, hailing every light they saw. At length they observed a large ship, and after chasing her for about five miles the Fire Queen came alongside, but only to the disappointment of the officers, for the vessel turned out to be a Prussian man-of-war. The Fire Queen then, at two o'clock on Tuesday morning, hailed a ship about ten miles this side of St. Catherine's, and she turned out to be the Victoria; they made a signal for her to stop, as they wanted to board her. The Victoria hove to, and Captain Huntley, of the Fire Queen, Langley, Thornton, and a local officer named Leggatt, went on board. They had a private interview with the captain, and he informed the officers that there were two persons on board named Manning, but he did not know who they were. After about one hour and a half search they found the berth, in which were two females sleeping, and were at once convinced that they were not the persons they were in search of. There were upwards of 270 emigrants on board. The Fire Queen then returned to Gosport.

APPREHENSION OF MARIA MANNING.

Maria Manning was arrested in Edinburgh, with a large amount of property belonging to the deceased, O'Connor, in her possession. On leaving Minver-place, she took in the cab with her three large boxes and a carpet bag. She first directed the cabman to drive to the London Bridge station of the South-Eastern Railway; having arrived there, she desired him to call a porter belonging to the railway, whom she requested to obtain some tacks in order to fasten some direction-cards (which in the course of the journey she had purchased, and on which she had written the assumed name of "Mrs. Smith") upon her boxes. This was done as directed, and two of the boxes, by the woman's desire, were conveyed into the luggage-office, with directions that they were to be taken care of until called for. The woman then re-entered the cab and was driven to the London and North-Western Railway station, were she alighted.

These circumstances having been communicated to Mr. Haynes, the superintendent of the detective police, that officer, at an early hour on Monday morning, the 20th of August, proceeded to the terminus of the South-Eastern Railway, where he fortunately found the boxes exactly as described, no inquiry having been made for them since they were deposited, on the Monday week previously. The suspicions entertained by Mr. Haynes now ripened into certainties, and he at once sought an interview with the secretary to the company, to whom he explained the whole matter, and urged the necessity of examining the contents of the boxes. Mr. Herbert conferred with two or three of the directors who happened to be at the station, and the Commissioners of Police having backed Mr. Haynes's application by a request to the same effect, the boxes were conveyed to the secretary's office, and there forced open. The first glance at each disclosed a quantity of female wearing-apparel, which, upon examination, proved to be marked with the name of "Maria Roux," the maiden name of Mrs. Manning.

further examination discovered a quantity of articles belonging to the deceased, Patrick O'Connor, and several letters written by him to the supposed murderess.

Mr. Haynes proceeded to the London and North-Western station, with the view of tracing Maria Manning. His inquiries here were fortunately most successful. In brief, we may state that he ascertained that a female passenger, whose luggage was marked with the name of Smith, had left the Euston station, on the morning of Tuesday, the 14th of August, by the 6h. 15m. A.M. train, having booked her place through to Edinburgh. There could be no longer any doubt as to the direction the suspected woman had taken, and Mr. Haynes, at ten minutes to one o'clock, telegraphed through to Edinburgh direct, addressing the superintendent of the city police, and informing him of the circumstances above detailed, with a full description of the suspected party. Mr. Haynes had scarcely arrived at Scotland-yard on his return when a messenger from the telegraph office reached there, bearing intelligence that Maria Manning had been arrested by Mr. Moxhay, the chief officer of the Edinburgh constabulary, upon the information forwarded by Mr. Haynes. The activity displayed by this officer may be judged of from the fact that scarcely an hour elapsed between the message being sent and the reply communicating the intelligence of the woman's arrest. At a later hour on Tuesday evening another telegraphic message was received from Edinburgh, communicating the result of the search made of the prisoner's person and luggage, from which it appears that the following property was found upon her:—73 sovereigns in gold, one £50 note, and six £10 notes, five of these latter bearing the numbers advertised as having been paid to Manning on Saturday, the 11th of August, on the presentation of one of the deceased's checks. In addition to this money, there were also found in the woman's possession all the missing scrip of the Sambre and Meuse and Boulogne and Amiens Railways, known to have been in the possession of deceased, and some articles of wearing-apparel belonging to him.

The particulars of Mrs. Manning's arrest are as follow:—It appears that the prisoner arrived in Edinburgh on the 15th or 16th of August, from Newcastle, and took lodgings with a woman of the name of Mrs. Hewat, in Haddington-place. She assumed the name of "Mrs. Smith." On the Friday she made a small purchase at the shop of a draper in the High-street, and, in the course of conversation, she asked the shopman if he would acquaint her with the name of some respectable sharebroker in Edinburgh. He accordingly directed her to the office of Messrs. Hughson and Dobson, sharebrokers, Royal Exchange. She did not immediately call upon these gentlemen, but reserved her visit to the following day. On calling on Saturday, she had a conversation with one, and subsequently with both the partners. She represented to them that she had dealt in Spanish bonds, and that she held at present some shares in the Amiens and Boulogne Railway, and also in the Sambre and Meuse Railway, which she said she would dispose of if she could do so to any advantage. Messrs. Hughson and Dobson informed her that foreign stock was not much dealt in about Edinburgh, but added that they had no doubt they could negotiate the sale of the stock through their London agent. She also informed them that she had in her possession from £300 to £500 in money, which she was much inclined to invest in Railway preference stock; and, in alluding to this matter, she expressed an anxiety to know if the dividends would be payable abroad. Messrs. Hughson and Dobson gave her every information on this subject, and at the same time told her, in the most friendly manner, that it was unsafe for her to travel with so much money about her, and that it would be better, in the meantime, for her to lodge it in some of the banks, from which she could draw it, with interest, when she met with an investment that should come up to her expectations. To this she replied, in a slightly foreign accent, and pointing at the same time to her breast, "I keep it here, where it's quite safe." In the course of the conversation, she further stated that she had come to Edinburgh within the last few weeks; that she was highly pleased with the city as a place of residence; and that she had enjoyed with great zest the sea-bathing at the neighbouring town of Portobello. She also represented that her father, to whom she gave the name of Robertson, resided in Glasgow, and that he had done a great deal of business, as well as lost a great deal of money, in railway shares. During the conversation she exhibited much animation and a great flow of spirits. It was ultimately brought to a close by her handing Messrs. Hughson and Dobson a scrip certificate, representing a certain number of shares in the Huntingdon, St. Ives, and Wisbeach Railway Company, upon which, it appeared, that £1 per share had been returned; and on her expressing a desire to learn if any further return was to be made upon these shares, Messrs. Hughson and Dobson undertook to correspond with their agent in London, and to give her information on the subject in the course of a day or two. She accordingly left the scrip certificate, on receiving a receipt for it; and before leaving she left them a note of her address.

On Monday she again called at the office of Messrs. Hughson and Dobson. The latter of these gentlemen only happened to be in the office at the time. After a few minutes conversation, she stated that she wished to have the scrip certificate of the Huntingdon, St. Ives, and Wisbeach Railway Company back again. She did not assign any reason for this; but she subsequently declared that it was either her intention to go that afternoon, or next morning, to Newcastle, to see her mother, who, she alleged, was unwell, and, with a smile, she said "of course she must pay every attention to her beloved parent." It was her purpose, however, she remarked, to return in a few days to Edinburgh. Mr. Dobson immediately gave her the scrip certificate, as she desired, when she tore up the receipt which she had received in lieu of it on the Saturday. Before going away she wished also to get back the name and address which she had left on her first visit. This, however, was not at hand at the time, and very fortunately, too, as it subsequently was the means of tracing her out, and leading to her capture so promptly.

On Tuesday morning, Messrs. Hughson and Dobson received a printed letter, acquainting them that certain shares in some foreign railways had been stolen in London, and cautioning them against having dealings in regard to them. This immediately excited their suspicions as to their fair visitant, and, after weighing and deliberating upon the matter, they became more and more convinced that "Mrs. Smith" must, in some way or other, have been connected with the nefarious transaction alluded to. Without a moment's delay. Mr. Dobson proceeded to the police office, and acquainted Mr. Moxhay, the superintendent, with the suspicions entertained by himself and his partner, Mr. Hughson. Mr. Moxhay consulted a description he had received of the person of Mrs. Manning, as well as that given in the London papers, and he at once became convinced, like Messrs. Hughson and Dobson, that "Mrs. Smith" was in reality Mrs. Manning. As a train was just about this time to start for Newcastle, they proceeded, in the first instance, to the station of the North British Railway Company, where Mr. Dobson, in company with Mr. Moxhay, personally inspected the passengers in all the carriages, but without discovering "Mrs. Smith." From thence they instantly went to the house of Mrs. Hewat, where "Mrs. Smith" had stated that she lodged; Mr. Dobson, having, luckily, before calling upon Mr. Moxhay, found the piece of paper on which the address of "Mrs. Smith" had been written. On arriving at the house of Mrs. Hewat, Mr. Moxhay, and a criminal officer who accompanied him, knocked at the door, and asked if a "Mrs. Smith" resided within, when they were answered in the affirmative, and were shown into her room, followed by Mr. Dobson. Mr. Moxhay appealed to Mr. Dobson if this was the woman that wished to dispose of certain railway stock to him, when that gentleman immediately answered in the affirmative. Mr. Moxhay then acquainted "Mrs. Smith" with the crimes of which she was charged. She made no answer. She was evidently, however, in a state of some excitement, but not at all equal to what might be expected from a party in her position. Her face became deadly pale, and she bit her lip and showed other symptoms of uneasiness.

Her luggage, consisting of two boxes and a carpet-bag, was then examined by Mr. Moxhay and the criminal officer, when the most undoubted evidence was obtained that the prisoner was no other than Mrs. Manning, and that she had in her possession the greater part of the property said to have been stolen from the house of Patrick O'Connor, who was so brutally murdered in London. The prisoner asked permission to retire into an adjoining apartment for a few minutes; but this being refused, she consoled herself by taking a glass of wine, and she repeated the draught more than once during the time that the examination of her baggage was going on. The wine inspired her with renewed confidence, and in a short time all her coolness and self-possession had returned. She was conveyed from her lodgings to the police-office in a cab; after which, intimation was sent to London, by telegraph, of her apprehension.

On Wednesday morning Maria Manning was placed at the bar of the Edinburgh police-court, according to the usual form observed in all such cases.

She walked into the dock with a firm, unfaltering step; and, during the whole time she was at the bar, her countenance did not betoken the slightest symptom of agitation or alarm. Ever since her apprehension, indeed, she has conducted herself in a manner that shows she is determined to brave all consequences, and not to give the slightest hint or indication that may, at a future period, tell against herself or her alleged husband and confederate in the murder. She was very neatly dressed; and, from her easy and graceful manner, she is evidently a person who has mixed a good deal in society. She is not, however, by any means what may be styled beautiful, as some of the papers have asserted. There is a kind of dogged expression about her face, which, when conjoined with the bold and somewhat callous manner at the bar of the police-court, and during the reading of the very serious charge against her led not a few of the on-lookers to say that she was just such a woman as could assist in the devising and carrying out such a deed as that in which, she is implicated.

Mr. Moxhay read the charge against her, which was in the shape of a petition at his own instance, and was as follows:—"The petition of Richard John Moxhay, superintendent of police, and procurator-fiscal of court for the public interest, humbly showeth—That your petitioner has been credibly informed that Maria Roux, or Reu, or Rieux, or Manning, at present in custody, has been guilty, actor or act in part, of the crime of murder; as also of the crime of theft; in so far as, upon the 9th of August, 1849, or about that time, the said accused did, within the house situated in Minver-place, New Weston-street, parish of Bermondsey, in or near London, then occupied by Frederick George Manning, wickedly and feloniously attack and assault Patrick O'Connor, residing in Greenwood-street, Mile-end, in or near London, and did discharge a pistol or other fire-arm, loaded with gunpowder and a leaden bullet, at the said Patrick O'Connor, whereby the said bullet penetrated and was lodged in his head; and also did with a hammer, or other lethal weapon to the petitioner unknown, strike him one or more blows on or near his head, by all which, or part thereof, he was mortally wounded, and died soon thereafter, and was thus killed by the said Maria Roux, or Reu, or Rieux, or Man-

ARREST OF MRS. MANNING, IN EDINBURGH.

ning; like as (2nd) upon the 10th day of August, 1849, or about that time, the said accused did wickedly and feloniously steal, and that unduly take away from the house situated in Greenwood-street aforesaid, lately before occupied by the said Patrick O'Connor, scrip of the Boulogne and Amiens Railway, of the following numbers:—48,665, 48,666, 48,667, 48,668, 48,669, 48,670, 48,671, 48,672, 48,673, and 48,674; and scrip of the Sambre and Meuse Railway, of the following numbers:—6460, 6461, 6462, 6463, 6464, 6465, 6466, 6467, 6468, and 6469; the property of the representatives or representative of the said Patrick O'Connor, whose name or names is or are to the petitioner unknown."

Sheriff Arkley, who was the presiding judge, said: Mrs. Manning, this a very serious charge against you, and it is my duty to tell you that it is not necessary that you should say anything, unless you please.

The prisoner, in a low but distinct voice, said, "I have nothing to say."

She was then removed from the dock to be sent to London, in the afternoon, by the Caledonian and North-Western Railways.

On her arrival on the Friday morning, she was taken to the Southwark Police Station. In the course of the morning she was brought before the magistrate at the Southwark Police Court, and, after a preliminary investigation of the circumstances, committed to Horsemonger-lane Gaol.

APPREHENSION OF MANNING.

The prevailing impression on the public mind was that Manning had made his escape to the Channel Islands, and was concealed there, and these are the circumstances which led to that conclusion:—First, he was known to have gone there on a former occasion when it was advisable to be out of the way; secondly, Mr. Bainbridge, the broker who bought the furniture, states that he slept at his house on Tuesday, August 14th, that next morning, he was greatly alarmed at the window-blinds being pulled up, because, as he said, he had a £200 bill falling due that day, and that he left suddenly in a cab. Thirdly, the cabman who took him from Mr. Bainbridge's house states that he set him down at the South-Western station, that he was directed by him to drive there by back streets and a circuitous route, and that he urged him to be quick, or he (Manning) would be too late. Lastly, an official communication was received from the Channel Islands, stating that a young woman had recognised him on board the steamboat going thither, she not knowing of the murder at the time, and that he had gone on to Jersey, while she landed at Guernsey.

Manning arrived at Southampton about two o'clock on Wednesday, the 15th August, and took up his quarters at the Oxford Arms Inn, near the railway terminus. Here he remained the whole afternoon, and at midnight left for Jersey by the South-Western Steam-packet Company's mail ship the *Despatch.*

During the voyage he appeared on deck very little, confining himself to the fore-cabin, and drinking brandy immoderately. On reaching Jersey he disembarked; and, in company with a fellow-passenger named Turk, with whom he had contrived to scrape acquaintance, walked into the town of St. Helier's. Arriving at the Navy Arms Inn, near the harbour, he walked into the house; and, with Mr. Turk, applied for the usual accommodation. Mrs. Berry, the landlady, happened to have only one double-bedded room disengaged; and this apartment having been offered to the two applicants, was accepted—Manning agreeing to pay 3s. per week for the rest of the room. On Thursday he went out in company with Mr. Turk to see the island, as he described it. He returned home in the evening and partook of tea with the landlord and the landlady, subsequently joining the company in the parlour, and entering freely into conversation with all who came into the room. There was a peculiarity about him which was not at all agreeable to the landlord, and was even less liked by the company. He was particularly overbearing in his manner, and frequently got into altercation with the parties to whom he addressed observations. Mr. Turk, the individual who accompanied him to the Navy Arms Inn, among the rest. During Saturday, Manning went out as usual, returning in the evening to the Navy Arms; and on the following morning he asked the landlord where he could go to church. In the course of the day he had a great deal of conversation with Mr. Berry, telling him that he had lost all his money in the French revolution, and that he must go to Paris to settle his affairs. He inquired what it would cost to go to Granville, the opposite port on the French coast, and upon ascertaining that he could go for about 20s., he expressed an intention of doing so, and begged that Mr. Berry, who, we should add, is a seafaring man, would accompany him as interpreter. Mr. Berry declined, and advised Manning, if he wanted to go to Paris, to return to London and go by the usual route to that capital, to which he seemed to accede, desiring to be called in time for the packet leaving Jersey on the following morning. He was roused, but declined to get up, and Mr. Turk having left Jersey on this day, Manning remained the occupant of the double-bedded room alone. He seldom dined at home, but took two or three meals a day in the house, and always ate most voraciously—to use the landlord's own words, " as much as three ordinary men."

On the Sunday morning, Manning entered the parlour of the Bath Hotel, kept by Mr. Somebody, one of the most respectable hostelries at St. Helier's, and joined in conversation with several tradesmen there assembled. The same overbearing manner which had rendered his company so disagreeable at the Navy Arms, distinguished him here. In the course of the evening he complained bitterly of the difficulty of obtaining good living in Jersey, and said he had had but one good dinner since he had been on the island, and that was off a collar of veal. He added that he ought not to feel surprised, for before he left town his brother clerk had said to him, with an oath, "Fred, my boy, you'll find the Jersey people a set of humbugs." The supercilious tone the fellow adopted in making this observation was not very gratifying to the persons assembled, and one of them, named Purkiss, who, it will be seen, subsequently took an active part in his apprehension, sarcastically replied, "I'll tell you what, sir, you'd find Jersey a very healthy place, for where there is one die there are twenty bolt." Manning, still in the same supercilious tone, rejoined, "What do you mean by bolt, sir?" upon which Manning threw himself back in his chair and laughed heartily. In the course of the evening, a gentleman present having mentioned that he came from Derby, Manning asked him if he knew the family of Massey, of Swarkstone, near that place, and, with a singular fatality, he went on to explain that the old gentleman's son had lodged with him in London while walking the hospitals; that he was a sad dog; and, suiting the action to the word, he took up his hat, and said, "Look here, the fellow changed hats with me before he left my house, and here is his name in the one I wear." This conversation, it must be recollected, took place before any news of the Bermondsey murder had reached Jersey, although it was known in London, the newspapers published on Saturday (in which the account first appeared) not reaching Jersey until the Tuesday following. During the remainder of the evening, Manning preserved the same swaggering manner, boasting of his position, and describing himself as a traveller for a cloth warehouse. One gentleman, more sceptical than the rest, expressing himself doubtful of something that Manning had said, he, in a domineering tone and manner, pulling at the same time from his pocket a large card, said, "If you are not satisfied, here's my card." He, however, took care not to exhibit the card. While at the Bath Hotel on this evening, he drank a quantity of brandy and water; and when the company broke up he was rather intoxicated. He had previously said that he was staying at the Union Hotel; and when he left the house, Mr. John Henlin, who subsequently took part in his apprehension, observing that he turned in a wrong direction for the Union, said, "I beg your pardon, sir, but I think you are going out of your road." Manning turned round and replied, "I know perfectly well where I have got to go to. Good night." On the afternoon of the following day he called again at the Bath Hotel, and asked Mrs. Seward's permission to walk into the bar-parlour. She allowed him to do so, and, seating himself in a chair, he entered into conversation with her. The want of tact he again exhibited while talking to Mrs. Seward was, it will be seen, most extraordinary; had he desired to secure his own apprehension he could scarcely have taken a more likely course to obtain it. He began by describing himself as a traveller for Sir R. Burnett's British gin, and spoke in high terms of Sir Robert's establishment. Mrs. Seward, knowing that her husband obtained his gin from Sir R. Burnett, was naturally surprised at this statement, and she at once told him that Mr. Seward obtained all the gin he had from Mr. Mann, the agent for Sir Robert, on the island. Manning, without exhibiting any alarm at this fact, threw himself back in the chair, laughed heartily, and exclaimed, "How very strange! My name is Mann——;" and then, stopping short, Mrs. Seward did not catch the last syllable. He remained for some length of time, spoke of the island as a most delightful place, and said he should bring his dear wife with him the next time he came. He also took occasion to tell Mrs. Seward that his wife was a very fine woman —that she was passionately fond of him, and that she always addressed him as her "dear Fred." Before leaving the Bath Hotel, Manning ascertained that Mr. Seward was in England, but that he would return on the following morning (Tuesday). He said he should be glad to make his acquaintance, and would call the next morning, and have a grilled fowl for lunch, which Mrs. Seward promised to get ready.

On the evening of this day, while walking in the streets of St. Helier's, Manning met a gentleman whom he formerly knew at Taunton, and who was staying at Jersey, passing his honeymoon. The gentleman observed Manning first, and, not wishing to recognize him, turned his head away before the other saw him. It is supposed that Manning, having remarked his presence on the island, felt that it would be unsafe to remain in St. Helier's, and determined to go further inland. He kept his appointment, however, at the Bath Hotel, on the following day, arriving about eleven o'clock. He was observed by the landlady to look into the parlour, where the cloth was laid for lunch. Mr. Parsons, the late clerk of the Hampton race-course, with another gentleman, was seated in the room at this time, and whether Manning recognized the face or not is uncertain, but, after looking into the room, he hastily withdrew, and was seen no more at the Bath Hotel.

The landlord of the Navy Arms, where he lodged up to this time, states that he noticed a remarkable change in his manner after Monday, and this alteration was also remarked and observed upon by the company who met him in the parlour on the evenings of each day. On the Sunday afternoon Manning hailed the driver of the St. Aubin's omnibus in St. Helier's, and, taking his seat on the box, rode along the coast in the direction of St. Lawrence. He talked freely to the driver, a man named Phillips, during his ride, and remarked on the beauties of St. Peter's Valley, through which they passed. On arriving at the hamlet of St. Lawrence, he waved his hand in token of recognition to a gentleman whom he, walking by the roadside. The gentleman, not recognising him as a friend, failed to acknowledge the salute, upon which Manning said to the driver, "Is not that gentleman's name Ford?" The driver replied that it was, and that he lodged at the British Lion, a small roadside inn, near at hand. Manning hereupon exclaimed, "Dear me, how very odd! he is a most particular friend of mine; I knew him intimately four or five years ago." The omnibus proceeded on its journey through the valley, and, on its return, brought Manning back as far as the British Lion, where he alighted. On entering the house, he immediately went up to Mr. Ford, who was seated near the entrance, and said, "Ah, Ford, my dear fellow, how do you do? I am so glad to see you." Mr. Ford at once recognized the person who addressed him as Manning, and recollected having frequently met him at the Globe, in South Audley-street, where Manning's sister formerly lived barmaid, and where she was visited by her brother. Mr. Ford having shaken hands, Manning invited himself to dinner, and actually did remain and dine with Mr. Ford and a widow lady who keeps the house. During dinner he spoke freely to Mr. Ford, and appeared quite at ease. After dinner he asked Mr. Ford if he understood the French language. Mr. Ford said he did slightly; upon which Manning begged that he would accompany him to France, as he wanted to go there to arrange several matters relating to some property. He said he would pay all expenses, and be very much obliged to Mr. Ford if he would go. Mr. Ford declined, and, entertaining some suspicion as to Manning's honesty, he asked him, "Are you married, Mr. Manning?" Manning replied, "Yes." Mr. Ford said, "Where is your wife?" Manning rejoined, "Oh, she is in London. The fact is, I have £200 or £300 to lay out, and I have come here to see how I can invest it best. When I have determined upon a course, I shall return to England and fetch my wife." He added that he was then in treaty for the purchase of a brewery at St. Helier's. Mr. Ford asked him whose brewery? Upon which Manning remarked that he was not at liberty to give the name at present. In the course of the afternoon, Manning expressed a strong desire to see Mr. Ford on the following day. Mr. Ford said he was engaged on the Monday and Tuesday, and ultimately an appointment was made for the following Wednesday, when Manning promised that he would dine with Mr. Ford at his lodgings. He came at the hour appointed on that day, but Mr. Ford, not being at all anxious to renew his acquaintance with his quondam friend, was not at home, at which Manning expressed some surprise, and asked whether he had not left a message for him. The landlady said he had not; and ultimately Manning remained to dinner with this lady and her daughter, and, in the course of an hour or two, left, as was supposed, for St. Helier's.

Within about three hundred yards of the British Lion, on the same line of road, stands a neat little cottage, over the door of which are inscribed the words "Prospect House," the windows looking directly into the bay of St. Aubin, and commanding a view of Queen Elizabeth's Castle, and all the picturesque scenery on that part of the coast. This house is occupied by an aged couple, natives of Jersey, named Berteau—the old man tilling a little land, and his wife increasing her store by letting lodgings. Two rooms in the house are occupied by a carpenter and his wife, also natives of Jersey, named Weildon; and neither of the families speak more than a few words of English, generally conversing in the Jersey patois. To this house Manning appears to have gone after leaving the British Lion on Wednesday, and observing a bill in the window, he inquired what apartments they had to let. Madame Berteau showed him a large bed-room, which he ultimately hired at four shillings per week; and he arranged to take his meals with the wife of the carpenter, who was to make his bed and wash for him. Having promised to return the same night, he went away.

He arrived at M. Berteau's house about eight o'clock on Thursday morning, and was shown into his room by Madame Berteau, who told him that if he had any friends call upon him, he might receive them in her own parlour down-stairs. He thanked her for her civility, but said that he should not have any one call upon him, as no one knew him in Jersey. He had not been long in the house before he sent out for a bottle of brandy, of which he drank frequently during the day. He remained in-doors all day, took his meals with Mrs. Weildon, and conversed with her on various subjects. In the evening he went out into the garden at the back of the cottage, putting on, for the first time, a blue Guernsey frock and a green felt hat, and remained there some time talking to M. Berteau, who was pursuing his ordinary avocations. He drank the whole bottle of brandy on Thursday, and early on Friday morning sent for a second, which he consumed in the course of that day. The same course of living was pursued by him on Saturday and Sunday, without any suspicion on the part of M. Berteau as to whom he was harbouring. On Sunday, a friend of Madame Berteau came in to see her, and, having heard something of the habits of the lodger, she remarked that his conduct appeared to be very strange, adding, that she hoped he was not the perpetrator of a dreadful murder which had happened in England. Madame Berteau had heard nothing of the murder, and thought little of her friend's caution, and so the matter dropped for this day. Fortunately, however, Madame Berteau's friend was not the only person whose suspicions were excited by the conduct of the murderer. The brandy consumed by Manning was procured from the house of Mr. Henlin, a very respectable inhabitant of Jersey, who lives in a small house in Saint Peter's Valley. Mr. George Henlin, one of the sons of this man, had the task of serving the girl who fetched the brandy, and he also thought it remarkable that so large a quantity of liquor should be consumed at M. Berteau's, who he knew was a very temperate man himself. He asked the girl certain questions, and ascertained from her that the person who drank the liquor was a lodger, who confined himself to the house all day, and drank brandy, as he said, to keep the cholera away. Mr. Heulin having heard in St. Helier's that the murderer of Patrick O'Connor was supposed to be concealed in Jersey, at once suspected this to be the man, and determined to satisfy himself, if possible. With this view he watched daily for his appearance in the garden, where the girl had told him he generally went in the evening for a short time. He saw him on Sunday evening, and again on Monday night; and was the more assured that it was the man in question, in consequence of his evident desire to escape observation by pulling his felt hat over his face as he walked up and down the garden. It should be stated that the garden in question is an open piece of ground, and can be overlooked from the high road, as well as from many other points of view. On Monday evening Mr. Heulin made so distinct an observation of Manning, while the latter was digging in the garden, that he felt no doubt of the identity of the man. About an hour after, and just as it was becoming dusk, Mr. Heulin went to the back entrance of M. Berteau's house, determined to ask him who and what his lodger was, and what name he passed under. Mr. Heulin found Manning sitting with M. Berteau outside the back-door, in a little yard, smoking his pipe. On seeing Mr. Heulin, M. Berteau advanced a few paces towards him. Manning rose at the same time, and retreated into the house. Mr. Heulin put such questions as he thought necessary to M. Berteau, and communicated his suspicions to him. M. Berteau, who is in very weak health, was somewhat alarmed; but he was also unwilling to believe that his lodger was the suspected party. He said the man appeared a very nice gentleman, and had given the name of Jennings; that he certainly did not go out much, but that might be accounted for by the fact of his being unwell, and afraid of the cholera; and no doubt, when better, he would go out as usual. Mr Heulin was not satisfied, and at once proceeded to St. Helier's, in order to communicate with his brother (Mr. John Heulin) on the subject. When the latter heard his brother's suspicions, he felt perfectly satisfied that M. Berteau's lodger was no other than George Frederick Manning, and at once proceeded in quest of Langley, the officer who had just arrived in Jersey, and whom he met within a few paces of the Bath Hotel, where his brother had detailed the circumstances to him. Mr. Langley felt so satisfied of the correctness of Mr. Heulin's suspicions, that he directly took that gentleman to Mr. Chevalier, and urged the propriety of going over to St. Lawrence directly, and arresting the man. It being now past nine o'clock, Mr. Chevalier suggested that the man would, in all probability, be gone to bed, and that perhaps it might be as well to defer his arrest until the morning. Mr. Langley at once objected, remarking that delays were dangerous; and that, as they were now so near their mark, they had better hit upon it. Mr. Chevalier at once consented. The party, consisting of Mr. Chevalier, Mr. Langley, Mr. Lockyer, the two Messrs. Heulins, and Mr. Purkis, at once left St. Helier's for M. Berteau's cottage, to which our narrative must again recur for a few moments. While Mr. George Heulin and M. Berteau were conversing together, Manning, who had merely retired from their immediate observation, remained in the back kitchen, the door of which being open, he overheard all that passed. The moment Mr. Heulin had gone, Manning went up to M. Berteau in the back kitchen, and asked him who the man was he had been talking to, what he came for, and why he wanted to know his name? M. Berteau stated that, while asking these questions, Manning trembled from head to foot, and appeared scarcely able to articulate. The thought instantly occurred to him that he was harbouring a murderer; and as soon as he had satisfied Manning that the person who had asked him the question was a neighbour, and that his motives were only those arising from curiosity, he exclaimed to his wife, "That's a murderer!" In order to prevent, as far as possible, the man from destroying himself, or committing any other crime, he put away a hatchet and some pieces of rope which were lying about the house.

Manning, it appears, retired to bed as soon as Mr. Heulin had gone, and at about half-past nine the officers arrived. They alighted from their carriage about 200 yards on the St. Helier's side of M. Berteau's cottage, and walked thither on foot. By a previously concerted arrangement, Mr. Chevalier and Mr. George Heulin went round to the back of the house and explained to M. Berteau that they were now come to arrest his lodger on a charge of murder—an announcement which appeared to give both the old man and his wife very considerable satisfaction. It was agreed that Mr. Chevalier should return to the front of the house, and knock at the door, which M. Berteau promised to open, and that he should hand to Mr. Chevalier a lighted candle, with which he undertook to proceed up-stairs to Manning's room, the door of which, if found locked, was to be instantly burst open, and the party in bed overpowered. It was arranged that the Messrs. Heulin should remain outside the cottage and prevent the escape of Manning by the windows, of which there were three to his room alone. Mr. Lockyer and Mr. Purkis followed Mr. Chevalier, and close behind them was Mr. Langley, who could alone identify the murderer, with another lighted candle. Contrary to expectation, the door of the murderer's room was found ajar, so that on reaching the landing the officers entered immediately. Mr. Chevalier pushed the door open hastily, and, placing the candle he held in his hand on the table, he rushed towards the bed in which the man lay. At the same instant, Langley, who had merely caught a side glimpse of his face, cried out, "There's the man—seize him!" Lockyer and Purkis instantly seized both the murderer's arms, Mr. Chevalier having thrown himself upon the bed and thus disabled him from making any further resistance. The somewhat rough seizure to which he was subjected appeared to

HOUSE IN JERSEY, IN WHICH MANNING WAS ARRESTED.

give Manning some annoyance, and he cried out "Hallo! what are you about? Do you mean to murder me?" The moment he saw Langley, however, he recovered his composure, and said, "Ah, sergeant, is that you? I am glad you are come, I know what you are come about. If you had not come, I was coming to town to explain all. I am innocent!" He then asked, "Is the wretch taken?" alluding to his wife, as Langley supposed. The officer replied in the affirmative; upon which Manning remarked, "Thank God, I am glad of it;. that will save my life. She is the guilty party; I am as innocent as a lamb." Mr. Chevalier directed him to dress himself in the presence of the officers, and when he had done so he proceeded to handcuff him. Manning, as soon as he saw the irons, said, "I hope you are not going to handcuff me." Mr. Chevalier explained the necessity of doing so, upon which he held out his hands, which were immediately pinioned by Lockyer. Manning saw that all the property in the room belonged to him; and seven sovereigns having been found in his carpet-bag, he said they were all that was left of a sum of £12, which had been paid to him for his furniture by a man in London, "and that," he added, "was all the money I had to start with." Having been conducted out of M. Berteau's house, he was placed in the carriage which had brought over the officers, and conveyed back to St. Helier's. On his way, although no questions were asked him, he volunteered several observations in reference to the crime. Among the remarks, in allusion to his wife, he said he "hoped she would not destroy herself before he got to London, for, when there, he could soon clear himself." Again he said, "I suppose she must have £1500 upon her; at least, she ought to have. She has often told me that she would be revenged upon O'Connor." Mr. Chevalier here asked what she meant by being revenged? Upon which Manning rejoined,. "Why, he induced us to take the house in Minver-place, and to furnish it, on the understanding that he would come and live with us, which he did not do; and my wife got into a great rage, and said she would be revenged. I said, 'Don't be angry, dear;' and advised her to forget and forgive. O'Connor got off his agreement by paying a few weeks' rent. A little before this time my wife went to his house, and he showed her notes and railway coupons, and promised that he would leave her the greater part of his property under his will." After a pause, he added, "She frequently went to his house; and about a fortnight before the murder she invited him to come and dine with us, but he did not come. She wrote him another letter, asking him to dine with us on the fatal day. The dinner was laid up-stairs when he arrived. My wife asked him if he would not go down-stairs and wash his hands, as was his custom, before dinner. He replied 'Yes,' and immediately went down-stairs, followed closely by my wife. As soon as they reached the bottom of the staircase, my wife put one of her arms round O'Connor's neck, and with the other hand she fired a pistol at the back part of his head. O'Connor immediately fell dead. I fainted, and do not know what became of the body." Mr. Chevalier asked him if he had not seen a hole dug in his back kitchen? Upon which he said, "Oh yes, I had seen it, and I believed that it was intended for me. I believe my wife intended to murder me."

Mr. Chevalier and the detective officers having placed their prisoner in safe custody in the gaol, the former waited on Sir Thomas Le Breton, and informed him of the capture of the supposed murderer. Sir Thomas immediately came down to the prison, and directed that a close watch should be kept upon him. Before Sir Thomas left the gaol, the prisoner complained of indisposition, and the medical officer (Mr. Jones) having been sent for, recommended that he should be allowed to have some brandy and water, after which he speedily recovered himself, and retired to bed in good spirits.

THE VOYAGE TO ENGLAND.

At seven o'clock on Friday morning, Mr. Chevalier and the detective officers proceeded to the gaol, for the purpose of conveying the prisoner to the packet. He made a particular request that he might be allowed to walk through the streets of St. Helier's; and, as it was very early in the morning, Mr. Chevalier consented to allow him to do so, Langley and Lockyer walking on either side, and Mr. Chevalier immediately behind him. There were very few persons present at this hour in the streets, so that no inconvenience arose from this circumstance. Even at the pier where he embarked, there could not have been more than 300 spectators. When the officers got him on board, he was conducted to a separate cabin in the forecastle, where he remained, during the whole voyage, in the custody of the officers. The officers kept the cabin as private as possible, but it was quite out of their power to prevent some parties on board from gratifying their curiosity by obtaining a sight of the supposed murderer. Manning was highly delighted at the notice he excited; and with one woman he conversed for some time, remarking that he had "had two wives, and that was one too many." Captain Childers, the Commander of the *Despatch*, recognised him immediately he came on board, and told the officers that on the night he crossed, the 18th of August, he recollected his coming to him several times, and pressing him to drink brandy; in fact, at one period of the night his conduct was so troublesome that Captain Childers was obliged to ask the steward to get him to turn into his berth.

The *Despatch* steamed into harbour after a sail of eleven hours. Mr. Inspector Haynes here came on board to receive the prisoner, and a fly having been obtained, he was handcuffed to one of the officers and conveyed to the railway station, and subsequently brought on by a special engine.

The special train arrived at the Vauxhall station at ten o'clock precisely; and as it was feared, the telegraph having announced the prisoner's expected arrival, that a crowd might be assembled at the Waterloo station, the prisoner was removed from the carriage at this place, and conveyed by Inspector Haynes and Sergeant Langley to the Stone's-end police-station, where the charge against him having been entered by Inspector Yates, he was placed in one of the cells, and closely watched by two officers.

EXAMINATION OF THE PRISONERS AT THE SOUTHWARK POLICE COURT, SEPTEMBER 6th.

At half-past eleven o'clock the prison van left the station for Horsemonger-lane Gaol, to convey the prisoners to the court. An intimation had been previously forwarded to Mr. Keane, the governor of the prison, by Mr. Secker, requesting that he would permit the parties to have an interview of five minutes' duration, in the presence of the officers, if they desired it, before leaving the gaol, this course being adopted to prevent the occurrence of a "scene" in court—a result which there was too much reason to fear might follow upon their being confronted for the first time in the dock. Mr. Keane, in carrying out the magistrate's suggestion, caused Manning to be first brought from the ward in which he was confined to the hall of his own residence, where his wife was presently introduced to him. As she entered, Manning raised his hand somewhat theatrically, and frowned upon her. A pause ensued, during which neither of the prisoners spoke to each other. Mr. Keane, observing this, said to Mrs. Manning, "Have you anything to say to your husband, Mrs. Manning?" The female prisoner replied, in a firm voice, "No." Mr. Keane then addressed a similar question to Manning, who also replied negatively. The two prisoners were then conducted to the Government van and driven off to the police court. The absence of all feeling exhibited by both parties was especially remarked by the officials who witnessed the interview between the prisoners, but it was universally admitted that Manning appeared considerably more affected than his wife by the awful position in which they both stood. On the arrival of the van in the station yard, the female prisoner alighted first, and walked with a quick step into the cell appropriated for her reception. Manning followed his wife, in custody of two officers, and evidently endeavoured to assume a carelessness of demeanour which ill accorded with his anxious countenance.

Precisely at twelve o'clock the male prisoner was brought into court, and placed at one end of the dock. As he passed through the crowd he trembled slightly and appeared somewhat alarmed. When relieved from the pressure of the spectators, he recovered his composure, and, beyond a slight quivering of the muscles of the face, gave no indication of uneasiness. The two solicitors, Mr. Binns (for the husband) and Mr. Solomon (for the wife), having taken their places in the dock, Mrs. Manning was introduced. As she entered, the inconvenience arising from the crowd in the body of the court was at its height, and the noise appeared slightly to disconcert her. While Mr. Edwin was endeavouring to quell the disturbance, Mrs. Manning sat down, and conversed with the female turnkey in attendance upon her, resting her head upon her hand, and evidently endeavouring to avoid the the glance of her husband, who sat in the opposite corner of the dock, looking at her most earnestly. The disturbance, among the spectators increased rather than diminished, until Mr. Secker gave peremptory orders that a large number of persons near the doors should be ejected, in order to allow the remainder breathing room. Order having been at length restored, Mr. Edwin directed the prisoners to stand upon an elevated platform prepared for them.

Manning rose immediately ; but, instead of standing erect, he sat down upon the side of the dock, in a careless attitude, his feet being placed upon the platform, and his hands, in which he held his hat, resting upon his knees. He was dressed in a shabby blue paletot, buttoned closely up to the chin, and around his neck he wore a red check silk handkerchief, tied in what is generally understood as "flash style." Having no shirt-collar, the extraordinary formation, or rather malformation, of his neck and chin, was rendered peculiarly prominent. His countenance, as before stated, wore an anxious expression, and throughout the day it was remarked that he neither changed his position, nor spoke a word.

Mrs. Manning, on being called upon to stand up, rose from the seat she had occupied, but appeared unwilling to mount the platform. Mr. Edwin therefore directed the officer to assist her, but she still objected, and, with a significant smile upon her countenance, appeared to solicit permission to remain in the position she then occupied. She was genteelly attired in a black satin dress with visite en suite, trimmed with black lace, a white straw bonnet, and black lace veil. Her appearance was decidedly improved since the preceding Friday.; She maintained the same air of composure throughout the day which marked her conduct on that occasion. She appeared to pay the greatest attention to the evidence of the various witnesses, and occasionally suggested questions to her solicitor, to assist him in his cross-examination. One remarkable feature in her conduct was a total indifference to the presence of her husband, towards whom she occasionally directed a furtive and contemptuous glance.

The evidence brought forward was of a similar nature to that which had been given on the coroner's inquest ; and, after several remands, the prisoners were fully committed for trial at the Central Criminal Court.

OUTHWARK POLICE-COURT.—EXAMINATION OF THE PRISONERS.

... her conduct ...
... attention to the review of the various
witnesses, and ... in his cross-
examination. One remarkable feature in her conduct was her indifference to the presence
of her husband, towards whom she occasionally directed ... contemptuous glance.
The evidence brought forward was of a similar nature to that which had been given on
the coroner's inquest ; and, after several ... committed for
trial at the *Central Criminal Court.*

THE TRIAL.

The trial of Frederick George Manning and Maria his wife, charged with the murder of Patrick O'Connor, commenced on the morning of Thursday, October 25th, at an early hour. The approaches to the Central Criminal Court presented appearances of bustle and excitement. Persons who had been fortunate enough to secure the *entrée* began to arrive before eight o'clock, anxious to secure favourable places in the court; and by the time the doors were opened—shortly before nine—a very considerable number of persons had assembled. There was, however, very little excitement manifested out of doors at that early hour; but as the day advanced the number of idlers in the Old Baily increased, and by noon a considerable crowd had collected, and continued to throng the street until the adjournment of the Court.

Admission could only be obtained by tickets from the Sheriffs, and, as this regulation was strictly observed, it had the effect of preventing the confusion and annoyance which must have resulted from the overcrowding of the court. Under the directions of the Under-Sheriffs, Messrs. Millard and Wire, every portion of the court which could be made available for the purpose was appropriated to the accommodation of spectators; and soon after nine o'clock nearly every seat was occupied. Several ladies were present on the bench and in the body of the court, but the attendance of the fair sex was far less numerous than we have seen on occasions of less general interest. In the early part of the morning, the gallery—to which it was reported a high charge was made for admission—was very thinly tenanted; but as the day advanced the number of its occupants increased, though it appeared to be far from crowded. Indeed, this was the only part of the court which was not fully occupied. Several gentlemen, and one or two ladies, who could not obtain accommodation in other parts of the court, were provided with seats in the dock. There was, as is usual on similar occasions of interest, a very numerous attendance of gentlemen of the long robe. Among the distinguished visitors present we observed Lord Bowden, Lord Strangford, Count Colloredo, the Austrian Ambassador, Baron Koller, Secretary to the Austrian Embassy, the Swedish Minister and his Secretary, the First Secretary to the Prussian Legation, the Marquis of Hertfort, the Marquis Azeglio (the Sardinian *Chargé d'Affaires*), Admiral Dundas, M.P., Aldermen Sir W. Magnay and Carden, and Sheriffs Lawrence and Nicoll.

At five minutes after ten o'clock, the Lord Chief Baron (Sir F. Pollock), Mr. Justice Maule, and Mr. Justice Cresswell, accompanied by the Lord Mayor, and the usual civic officers, entered the court. At the same time, the two prisoners, Frederick George Manning and Maria Manning, were placed at the bar. The male prisoner was the first to enter the dock, in charge of Mr. Cope, the Governor of Newgate, and, advancing to the front, he took his place at the right-hand corner. The female prisoner, who immediately followed, walked to the other extremity of the dock; but no look or token of recognition was exchanged between them. Manning was attired in a respectable suit of black, and wore a black neckerchief. He appeared in better health and spirits than at his examination at the police-court; but during the day he manifested a nervous restlessness. He frequently changed his position at the bar, and was observed, on several occasions, to cast furtive glances at his wife. She, on the contrary, for more than an hour after she was placed in the dock, remained almost as motionless as a statue, and was never seen, throughout the day, to turn her eyes towards her husband. She seemed to be suffering from illness, and had lost the appearance of robust health which characterised her previously to her committal. The cheerful buoyancy of spirits, amounting almost to levity, which she manifested at the preliminary examinations, appeared also to have deserted her. She remained standing until the Judges had given their decision upon the application of her counsel for a trial *per medietate linguæ*, when, at the request of Mr. Ballantine, she was accommodated with a chair. She wore a black or dark dress, fitting closely up to the throat, a shawl of somewhat gaudy colours, in which blue predominated, and primrose-coloured gloves. She was without bonnet, and wore as a head-dress what appeared to be a very handsome white lace veil.

The male prisoner is described in the calendar as thirty years of age, and by trade a "traveller;" and his wife as "married," and twenty-eight years of age. Both the prisoners, however, appear much older.

The Attorney-General (Sir J. Jervis), Mr. Clarkson, Mr. Bodkin, and Mr. Clerk appeared for the prosecution, instructed by Mr. Maule, the solicitor to the Treasury; Mr. Sergeant Wilkins and Mr. Charnock were for the male prisoner, and Mr. Ballantine and Mr. Parry for Mrs. Manning.

The prisoner Frederick George Manning, was charged on the indictment (which was read by Mr. Straight, Clerk of Arraigns) with having, on the 9th of August, 1849, at Bermondsey, feloniously discharged a pistol loaded with a bullet at Patrick O'Connor, and inflicted upon him a mortal wound, of which he then and there died. The second count charged the said Frederick George Manning with having caused the death of Patrick O'Connor by striking, cutting, and wounding him on the back part of the head with a crow-bar. There were other counts alleging that the death of O'Connor had been caused jointly by the shooting and beat-

FREDERICK GEORGE MANNING.

MARIA MANNING.

ing, and describing the weapon used as an air-gun. Maria Manning was indicted for having been present, aiding and abetting the said Frederick George Manning to commit the felony.

On being called upon to plead, the male prisoner explained, in a loud and firm tone, "Not guilty."

Mr. Ballantine said he appeared on behalf of Mrs. Manning, who was a native of Geneva, and who, as an alien, prayed that she might be tried by a jury composed partly of aliens.

The Chief Baron: The prisoner ought to plead before the application is made.

Mr. Ballantine would call their Lordships' attention to "Bacon's Abridgement," vol. 4, p. 568, where it was laid down that, "If upon an indictment of felony against an alien he plead 'Not guilty,' and a common Jury be returned, if he do not surmise his being an alien before any of the Jury sworn, he hath lost that advantage; but if he allege that he is an alien, he may challenge the array for that cause, and thereupon a new precept or venire shall issue, or an award be made of a jury de medietate linguæ. But it is more proper for him to surmise it upon his plea pleaded, and thereupon to pray it." If, however, it was their Lordships' opinion that the plea should be pleaded before the application was made, the female prisoner was now ready to plead.

The Chief Baron said, according to the old form, when the question was put, after the plea had been put in, "How will you be tried?" the prisoner, instead of answering "By God and my country," said, "By a Jury de medietate linguæ."

Mr. Ballantine: Then we will take the plea.

The usual question—"Are you guilty or not guilty of this felony?"—was then put to the female prisoner by the Clerk of Arraigns, and she replied, in a tone scarcely audible a few feet from the dock, "Not guilty."

The prisoners were then arraigned on the Coroner's inquisition, and both of them pleaded "Not guilty."

The clerk was proceeding to swear the Jury, when

Mr. Ballantine said: Mrs. Manning desires to be tried by a Jury de medietate linguæ, and prays your Lordships to award it.

The Attorney-General understood his learned friend to make this application on the ground that his client was technically and legally an alien.

Mr. Ballantine: I put it upon that ground.

The Attorney-General said, that, although aliens were undoubtedly entitled to that privilege, yet that Mrs. Manning, being the wife of a British subject, had no claim to a Jury de medietate linguæ. And, even if she were not the wife of a natural-born subject of this realm, yet, being tried upon a joint indictment, she would not be entitled to such a Jury. With regard to the first point, it was declared by the act 7 and 8 Victoria, chap. 66, sec. 16, "that any woman married, or who shall be married, to a natural-born subject or person naturalised, shall be deemed and taken to be herself naturalised, and have all the rights and privileges of a natural-born subject." But it had been expressly decided that, even if the female prisoner were now an alien to all intents and purposes, yet that, being indicted jointly with a natural-born subject, she was not entitled to a Jury de medietate linguæ. He would refer their Lordships to the abstract of Barre's case (Moore, 557), "Bacon's Abridgement," vol. 4, p. 557. It was there laid down that, "upon an information exhibited by the Attorney-General against several merchants, some of whom were aliens and some English, after issue joined, the aliens prayed a trial per medietate linguæ, but it was resolved by all the Judges of England that they should not have it; and they likened it to the case of privilege where one of the defendants demands privilege, and the Court (as his companion) cannot hold plea, there he shall be ousted of his privilege."

Mr. Ballantine said he had submitted his application partly upon a statute with which their Lordships were familiar, the 6th George 4, c. 50, sec. 47, which provides that nothing therein contained shall extend to deprive any alien indicted or impeached of any felony or misdemeanour of the right of being tried by a jury de medietate linguæ; but that, on the prayer of every alien so indicted or impeached, the Sheriff shall return for one-half of the Jury a competent number of aliens, if so many there be in the town or place where the trial is held; and, if not, then so many aliens as shall be found in the same town or place.

The Chief Baron asked the learned gentleman to assist the Court by going a little further back, and pointing out how an alien became at all entitled to a jury de medietate linguæ. He believed it was by a statute of Edward III.?

Mr. Ballantine: The 28th Edward III. But, though that statute might intimate the right of an alien to be tried by a jury of this kind, he thought it important to call the attention of the Court to the modern statute he had cited, to show that it contained a declaration that the rights of aliens should be perfectly carried out. In was, in fact, a re-enactment of the act of Edward III. by the Legislature, with the knowledge of any difficulties that might have arisen under the operation of that act. He thought it an important fact that no exception was made in the statute of George IV. The Legislature must have passed that statute with the knowledge that aliens had been indicted along with persons who were not aliens; and they were also perfectly well aware that aliens might marry natural-born subjects of this realm.

The Chief Baron: The act of 6th George 4 (Sir R. Peel's Jury Act) was passed long prior to the statute mentioned by the Attorney-General.

Mr. Ballantine: But, inasmuch as there was no express enactment in that statute with reference to a person placed in the particular position of the female prisoner, he apprehended that the prior act, which was perfectly clear, could not be overruled by the subsequent statute, and that the right could not be taken away by the mere implication of that statute. This was an extremely important privilege in the administration both of the criminal and civil justice of the country, and he thought their Lordships would be of opinion that it could only be abolished by express and direct enactment. He would call the attention of the Court to one or two other authorities, to show what had been deemed the rule from time to time. In "Comyns' Digest," tit. "Alien," D 1, it is stated that "the King only has the prerogative to make any alien to be a denizen; that he cannot grant this prerogative to any other; and that the usual manner of a denization is by letters patent, and so it may be by Parliament." He understood the Attorney-General to contend that the 7th and 8th Victoria, c. 66, rendered the law as it stood previously to that statute inoperative with reference to the female prisoner, in consequence of her being a married woman; and that that statute, by giving her all this rights of a natural-born subject, took away from her the power of demanding a jury *de mediatate linguæ*. He (Mr. Ballantine) apprehended, however, that a law which involved so important a right as that now claimed by the female prisoner could only be abrogated by express terms, and that there was nothing in the terms of the act cited by the learned gentleman to take away that right. He considered that the grounds upon which Barre's case, which had been referred to by the Attorney-General, was decided, were not at all applicable to the present case. The Chief Baron had asked him (Mr. Ballantine) to refer to the statute 28 Edward III., c. 13, and he found ("Bacon's Abridgement," p. 566) that that statute enacted, that "in all manner of inquests and proofs which be to be taken or made amongst aliens and denizens, be they merchants or others, although the King be party, the one-half of the inquest or proof shall be denizens and the other half aliens, if so many aliens and foreigners be in the town or place where such inquest or proof is to be taken; and if there be not so many aliens, then shall there be put in such inquests or proofs as many aliens as shall be found in the same towns or places, that be not thereto parties, and the remnant of denizens which be good men, and not suspicious to the one party nor to the other." He apprehended that the real question in this case was, whether the woman at the bar was a denizen, and, if not, he submitted that she was entitled to be tried by a jury *de mediatate linguæ*.

Mr. Parry followed on the same side. He contended that the privilege claimed by the female prisoner was one which could not be got rid of by mere implication in an act of Parliament; but that, if abolished at all, it must be abolished by express enactment. The 7th and 8th of Victoria, c. 66, conferred certain privileges upon aliens born, who married natural-born subjects of the Crown; but it did not take away any privilege that had been previously conferred by any act of Parliament; and he therefore submitted that the clause of that act upon which the Attorney-General relied did not support his objection, because it did not by express enactment take away the right claimed by the prisoner as an alien born. He apprehended that there was only only one way in which a person born an alien could divest himself of the capacity or *status* of alienage, and that was by the consent of the State or Government of which he was a subject. It had been decided in Doe *dem*, Thomas *v.* Acklom, 2 Barn. and Cress., 779, that the only way in which a natural-born subject could divest himself of that condition was by the consent of his liege lord.

Mr. Justice Cresswell: Was it not rather that a man cannot get rid of the allegiance he owes to the country where he was born?

Mr. Parry apprehended it was decided that a person could not divest himself of the condition of alienage without the consent of the country of which he was a natural-born subject. He would refer their Lordships to 4 Blackstone's Commentaries, page 352, where it was clearly laid down that the female prisoner was entitled to the privilege she now claimed. Speaking of challenges in criminal cases, Blackstone says, "Challenges may here be made either on the part of the King or on that of the prisoner; and either to the whole array, or the separate polls, for the very same reasons that they may be made in civil causes. For it is here at least as necessary as there that the sheriff or returning officer be totally indifferent; that where an alien is indicted, the jury should be *de mediatate*, or half foreigners, if so many are found in the place." The Court, he thought, would hardly hold, upon the authority of the case cited by the Attorney-General, that because the female prisoner was indicted jointly with a natural-born subject, she was thereby debarred from her privilege as an alien. These parties might have been indicted separately. Would their Lordships hold that, because a peer was jointly indicted with a commoner, his privilege of trial by his peers was taken away from him?

After a consultation between the Chief Baron and his brother Judges, which occupied nearly half an hour,

The Chief Baron announced the decision of the Court. He said that Frederick George Manning and Maria Manning his wife were indicted for murder, and both had pleaded not guilty. Maria Manning had suggested by her counsel that she was entitled to have a jury *de mediatate linguæ*, on the ground of her being an alien. The Attorney-General had opposed this application, and had cited Barre's case, which had occurred in the Court of Exchequer, and the statute of 7 and 8 Victoria, which enacts that an alien woman marrying a natural-born subject of this realm shall become naturalised by the marriage. It appeared to him (the

Chief Baron) that the statute of Victoria was an answer to the application. He would forbear going into the argument with reference to Barre's case, for he would not like hastily, and without much more consideration, to adopt the decision there given as applicable to the present case; but he considered that the statute of Victoria was a complete answer to the application which had just been made. By that statute an alien woman who married a natural-born subject became naturalised by the marriage; and from the terms of the statute it appeared to him that she would be considered exactly as if she had been naturalised by act of Parliament, or had been herself a natural-born subject. The question remains, whether she could now claim a Jury de medietate linguæ. Her husband, as a natural-born subject, could not be tried by a jury so constituted. The language of the statute of Edward III., and, indeed, of all the modern statutes explaining the law, was, that in all manner of inquests and proofs which be to be taken or made amongst aliens, although the King be party, one-half of the inquest shall be denizens and the other half aliens. Now, the question was, whether this was an issue to be taken between the Queen and an alien. Maria Manning had married a natural-born subject of the realm, and was deemed and taken to be naturalised. It was laid down by Hawk. P. C., book ii. chap. 43, sec. 39, "It is holden that by denizens in this statute are meant, not only those who are born within the King's liegeance, but also those who are made denizens by the King's letters patent." It had been contended by Mr. Parry that the statute of Victoria was intended to confer privileges and to create new rights, but not to take away privileges which had previously existed; but it appeared to him (the Chief Baron) that the answer to that was, that the status of the party was altered. All the privileges which were personal—which belonged to the individual—had been preserved; but the privilege of being tried by a jury de medietate linguæ was not the individual privilege of the prisoner, but of the status or condition to which he belonged. It was not necessary, then, to take away that privilege by express words; it was sufficient to alter the status of the person. The moment he ceased to be an alien, the inquest to be taken ceased to be an inquest between our Sovereign Lady the Queen and an alien, and became an inquest between the Queen and a naturalised subject of the realm. It appeared to the Court, therefore, that the trial must proceed.

Mr. Ballantine then moved that his application might be entered upon the record.

The Attorney-General said, if that were done, he would plead that the female prisoner had married Frederick George Manning, a natural-born subject of the realm.

After some conversation, it was agreed that Mr. Ballantine should have the option of raising the question on the record, or of having the point reserved for the consideration of the Court of Appeal in Criminal Cases.

The female prisoner paid great attention to the arguments upon this application of her counsel; but when the decision of the Court—adverse to her interests—was delivered, she did not exhibit the slightest emotion.

The Attorney-General then proceeded to state the case to the Jury. He said that the great importance of the investigation they were about to enter upon, and the excitement which it had created in the public mind, had induced him, as the public prosecutor, to appear to conduct the case; for he was desirous of taking upon himself any responsibility that might arise in connexion with the case; and his object would be simply to elicit truth, and to assist in the firm administration of justice. He was quite certain that, upon a charge of this serious nature—almost the most serious charge that could be made against any member of the community—it was unnecessary for him to caution the Jury to dismiss altogether from their minds—as he implored them to do—everything they had heard or read upon the subject of this painful event, and to confine their attention solely to the evidence which would be produced before them, and upon which alone, under the direction of the Court, they ought to arrive at their decision. He feared that it would be necessary for him to enter at some length into the details of the case; but he would abstain as much as possible from unnecessarily occupying their time. It would be his duty simply to lay before them, as shortly and clearly as possible, a statement of the circumstances which would be detailed in the subsequent evidence. The prisoners were Frederick George Manning, who, he believed, formerly came from Somersetshire, and who was for some time a guard in the service of the Great Western Railway Company, until 1847, when he married the female prisoner, Maria Manning. She was, he believed, a native of Switzerland. She had formerly lived in the service of a daughter of the Duchess of Sutherland—Lady Blantyre; and she was married to the prisoner in the year 1847. After that time these persons kept an inn at Taunton, and they subsequently took a house in Minver-place, Bermondsey, the scene of the fatal murder. Patrick O'Connor, whose death was the subject of this charge, was for many years a gauger in the Customs; and on Thursday, the 9th of August last, was stationed at the London Docks. He resided in Greenwood-street, Mile-end, at some distance from Minver-place. On Thursday, the 9th of August, Patrick O'Connor left his ordinary place of residence in Greenwood-street, about half-past seven in the morning. He was present at the London Docks at the ordinary time—eight o'clock. He signed the appearance-book. He remained on duty till four o'clock, when he again signed the departure-book, as having left his duty at that time. About a quarter before five o'clock he was seen by two friends near London-bridge, and, being questioned as to where he was going, he produced and showed to one or both of them a letter of invitation to dinner, which he said, and which was signed "Maria." About five o'clock on the same day he was seen in Weston-street, about three minutes' walk from Minver-place; and a little later he was again seen by another person on London-bridge, apparently hesitating which way he should go. That was the last occasion on which he was seen alive. On the 13th of August the two prisoners precipitately left their house, in the manner which he would subsequently describe. On the 14th of August their landlord found the house in which they had lived unoccupied, it having been left without notice; and on the 17th, the police, having obtained access to the house, made a diligent and careful search of the premises; and in the back kitchen, under the flagged pavement, at the depth of about four feet, was found the body of Patrick O'Connor, thrust into a hole, the legs being bound back to the haunches, covered with lime, and naked. No clothes of the deceased were found upon the premises; no letter of invitation to him to dinner; no instruments likely to have inflicted the wounds which had caused O'Connor's death. The body had been and would be clearly identified. Although, of course, the fact of finding the body of O'Connor under such circumstances in the house occupied alone by the two prisoners, was not to be taken alone as conclusive of the guilt of both or either of the prisoners, there could be no doubt that—the body being mutilated by a shot through the head, and the skull being fractured in a dreadful manner—by some party or other O'Connor was murdered between the 9th of August, when he was last seen alive, and the 17th of that month. He (the Attorney-General) thought his learned friends who were retained for the prisoners would have no right to complain, then, if he started with the assumption that this unfortunate man had been murdered on the premises; and he thought, also, that it was no unfair presumption to conclude that one or other of the prisoners had taken part in the dreadful act. He feared that, when the Jury heard the evidence to be adduced, they would be of opinion that the death of O'Connor was the result of a deep-laid plot; and the question for them to consider would be, whether both or either of the prisoners had been concerned in that plot. Before he proceeded to state to them the evidence, it was his duty to point out one or two legal principles which were applicable to the case. The Jury had heard of the charge in the indictment, which was laid in various ways. Frederick George Manning, the male prisoner, was charged with having actually committed the murder, by shooting the deceased, by striking him with a crow-bar, by both shooting and striking him, and by shooting him with an air-gun; and Maria Manning, the female prisoner, was charged with being present, and aiding and abetting in the commission of the act. The law required that the charge should be thus technically laid, but it did not require that it should be so technically proved. If the Jury should be of opinion that Maria Manning's was the hand that committed the fatal deed, and that the husband was present—though not actually present in the very room, but so far present as to be aiding and assisting in the act; nay, if it were supposed that some person not mentioned in the indictment had committed the murder, but that the male prisoner was present, aiding and abetting, he must be found guilty. The Jury, therefore, would not be encumbered by any technical inquiry as to whether it was the hand of the man or the woman that inflicted the deadly wound upon the deceased. If either of them committed the act, and the other was present, participating in the murder, both would be guilty of the charge. Formerly, there was another difficulty which might have been presented in an inquiry of this description. When dreadful crimes of this kind were committed, it was seldom that any one but the immediate actors were present; it was difficult to get actual and eye testimony of the commission of such offences; and juries were satisfied with that which he thought was in its nature sometimes even more satisfactory—not ocular, but circumstantial, though conclusive evidence. On some occasions it had been found necessary to ascertain whether all persons who were charged with offences of this description were actually, personally, and legally present at the time of their commission; for though those who concerted and counselled and effected a murder were, legally and morally, equally guilty and responsible for the consequence, the law formerly required that persons should be charged according to their actual degrees of guilt—principals as principals, and accessories as accessories; and if the Jury doubted whether persons were really present, legally and actually, at the time of the murder, though they might have concerted the murder, such persons were acquitted upon a technical objection. That, however, was provided against by a recent statute. The 11th and 12th Vict., c. 46, s. 1, enacted that those who were accessories before the fact to any felony, including murder, might be indicted and punished as principals; and the Jury in this case would therefore be relieved from all difficulty in considering whether Manning struck the deadly blow in the presence of his wife, or whether she committed the act with the previous knowledge of her husband. There was another legal proposition to which he wished to advert. The Jury were aware that, in some cases, the humanity of the law presumed that married women were under the coercion and constraint of their husbands; and there were some offences which, if committed by a married woman in the presence of her husband, were excused, by the indulgence of the law, and he alone was criminal. That rule, however, never did or ought to apply to offences which the law termed mala in se—those which were heinous and abhorrent to the laws of nature; and it never had been supposed that in the case of treason or murder juries should be encumbered by any question as to whether a woman, if present, was acting under the coercion of her husband. These were propositions to which he wished to call the attention of the Jury before he stated the facts. There was, however, one other matter which ought not to be passed over, because possibly his learned friends might advert to it in defending the prisoners. It might be alleged for the defence, that the offence, if committed by either of the prisoners, was committed by the man, and that the woman could be regarded only as a principal in the second degree—not as an accessory before the fact, but as an accessory after the fact. She was not so charged, nor could she be so charged; for the law did not allow any charge to be made against a married woman for being an accessory after the fact, for comforting and harbouring her husband; and he did not believe that the evidence in this case would warrant any such conclusion with regard to the female prisoner. Bearing in mind, then, the propositions he had stated, he thought it would be admitted that he was justified in assuming that Patrick O'Connor had been murdered by some one in the house occupied by the prisoners. The question for the Jury would be, was the murder committed by both the prisoners, or by either of them, in the presence, legal, actual, or constructive, of the other; or was it committed by either of them, with the guilty concert or connivance of the other, but in his or her absence? If either of these propositions was established to the satisfaction of the Jury, both the prisoners must be found guilty. He must now take the Jury back to the facts of the case, and would give them, chronologically, a history of the connexion between the parties. The origin of the intimacy between O'Connor and the Mannings he had been unable to trace, but he had reason to believe that, at some time previously to 1847, O'Connor had paid his addresses to the female prisoner. Recently, however, and for some time past, they had been upon terms of intimacy. The female prisoner was in the constant habit of visiting O'Connor, and she was on such terms of intimacy with him as not only to be acquainted with all his pecuniary affairs (he being a man of considerable property), but, by his direction, she was admitted to his apartments, where she remained frequently, in his absence, for a considerable time. At Lady-day last the prisoners became tenants of the house No. 3, Minver-place, Bermondsey. Some time afterwards, a gentleman named Massey, a medical student, became a lodger in their house. The prisoners kept no servant, the household work being generally done by the female prisoner herself, with the occasional assistance of a charwoman. In the presence of his wife, Manning several times made statements to and inquiries of Mr. Massey, which at the time seemed unimportant, but which appeared to him (the Attorney-General) of so much importance that he considered it his duty to call the attention of the Jury to them. Manning stated, in the presence of his wife, that O'Connor was a man of considerable property (about £20,000); and he was represented also to have said that O'Connor had made a will in favour of his wife. Manning made inquiries of Massey as to the effects of chloroform and laudanum, and whether they would be effective in stupifying a man so far that he might put his hand to a note for £500, which he (Manning) wished to obtain from O'Connor. Manning also inquired what was the most vital part of the human body, and was told the jugular vein. He asked where was the seat of the brain; and it was pointed out to him by Massey. Manning further inquired of Massey whether he had ever discharged an air-gun, and whether it made a noise; and upon another occasion, he asked him what he thought would be the end of a murderer. Massey, at the time, paid very little attention to these conversations, which took place about the end of July. Previously to the 28th of July, both the prisoners expressed their desire most anxiously that Massey should leave the premises. They said they were going out of town for a time; they pressed him over and over again; and on the 28th of July Massey left Manning's house, and went to Mr. Bainbridge's in Bermondsey-square. On the 23rd of July the male prisoner went to the house of a builder named Wells, where he purchased a bushel of lime, saying that he wanted it for the purpose of destroying slugs in his garden. B-ing asked whether he required grey lime or white lime, he said, the lime he wanted was that which would burn the quickest, and, accordingly, grey lime was sent. Manning made a bargain with Mr. Wells's boy, to give him something for taking the lime to his house. Accordingly, when the boy took the lime to the house, the door was opened by the female prisoner, who, without saying anything or hearing anything from him, as to whether he expected to be paid for his trouble, gave him some money, and the male prisoner pointed out to him a basket in which it was to be shot. On the 25th of July the male prisoner ordered, at a shop in King William-street, a large crow-bar, which was to be made, by agreement, for a certain sum. The crow-bar was made, and was delivered on the 28th of July. The man who was directed to take it home, carried it in his hand, without any wrapper. About the middle of London-bridge he was met by Manning, who complained that the crow-bar was not wrapped in paper, and took the man to a stationer's in Tooley-street, where he (Manning) purchased a quantity of paper, covered up the crowbar, and then directed the messenger to take it to Minver-place, where he said a person would be to receive it. The man went to Minver-place, where the door was opened by the female prisoner. The man said nothing, but gave her the crow-bar, which was covered with paper. She asked him the price, and when he informed her, she complained that it was more than had been bargained for. She, however, paid him the money, and received the crow-bar, still wrapped in paper. Now he (the Attorney-General) must remind the Jury that, when the body of O'Connor was found, the crow-bar was not discovered upon the premises, nor was it among the articles which had been sold to a broker. On the 8th of August—the day preceding that on which O'Connor was last seen alive—Mrs. Manning purchased a shovel, stating that she wanted a stout one, and that it was immaterial whether the handle was long or short. On the 8th of August, then, after the purchase of the lime, the crow-bar, and the shovel, Mrs. Manning wrote a letter to O'Connor, asking him to dine at the house that day, in these terms:—

> "Wednesday morning.
> "Dear O'Connor,—We shall be happy to see you to dine with us to-day, at half-past five.
> "Yours, affectionately,
> "MARIA MANNING."

This note was posted on the 8th of August, at three o'clock in the afternoon, and was addressed to O'Connor at the London Docks; it would not, therefore, be delivered until the following day, and was evidently not the letter which O'Connor had shown to his friends upon the bridge. Indeed, this note was delivered at O'Connor's house the following day (the 9th) by a porter from the docks, O'Connor having left home at half-past seven in the morning. On the evening of the day when that letter was sent (the 8th of August) O'Connor went to the house of the Mannings, happily, in company with a gentleman named Walshe. Mrs. Manning said she had written a letter to ask him to dinner, and was surprised he had not come. O'Connor replied that he had not received the letter. O'Connor stayed at Manning's house that night till about twelve o'clock, smoking, but not drinking, and some conversation took place as to some money which Mr. Walshe had received for him. At twelve o'clock O'Connor left, having complained during the evening of being unwell. On the 9th he went to the Docks, and left them at four o'clock. He was seen that evening on London-bridge, again in Weston-street, near Minver-place, and again, when he seemed undecided where to go, and from that time he was not seen again alive. About a quarter to six o'clock on the evening of the 9th, the female prisoner went to the house of O'Connor, in Greenwood-street. He (the Attorney-General) had instructed persons to ascertain the period of time that would be occupied in going from Minver-place to the lodgings in Greenwood-street. He found that to walk the distance would occupy about forty-two minutes, and to go by omnibus thirty-five minutes, and by cab about twenty-five minutes. Mrs. Manning stayed at Greenwood-street that night until about a quarter-past seven o'clock. The male prisoner was certainly in Minver-place that evening, for about a quarter-past seven o'clock he was seen smoking and chatting upon the wall at the back of the premises, where he remained about twenty minutes, and then suddenly jumped down, and went away abruptly, saying that he had to keep an engagement. On the 10th of August, the day following that which they might reasonably conclude to have been the day of the murder, Mrs. Manning again went to the house in Greenwood-street, about a quarter to six o'clock, and remained there about the same time she had done the previous evening; and he thought it was not unfair to presume that she had gone there for the purpose of removing part of O'Connor's property. Her visit excited no suspicion, for, as he had said, she was in the constant habit of going to the house; but the witnesses observed that when she left she appeared nervous and pale. The 10th of August was on Friday. On the 11th Mrs. Manning engaged a girl to clean the back and front kitchen in Minver-place, and also directed her to clean a basket in the back kitchen, which appeared to have been filled with lime. The girl was unable to clean the basket, and Mrs. Manning endeavoured to do so herself, until she had exhausted all the water on the premises. On the same day, the 11th, the male prisoner went to a stockbroker's, where, in the name of Patrick O'Connor, he sold, for £110, twenty of the Eastern Counties Railway shares, which were unquestionably the property of O'Connor. Manning received for them a £100 note, which was changed at the Bank for fifty sovereigns and five £10 notes; and the notes thus given in change were afterwards found in the possession of Mrs. Manning. The absence of O'Connor from his ordinary duties had naturally created suspicion and uneasiness among his friends; and on Sunday, the 12th, the persons who had met him on London-bridge on the 9th called at the house of the prisoners, where they saw the woman, and asked if she had seen O'Connor, and whether he had dined there on the Thursday previously? She said no—that she had not seen him since the previous Wednesday, when he had visited her with Mr. Walshe. She said she had expected him on Thursday, and had called at his house to inquire for him. Mr. Walshe was not satisfied with this statement; and on the Monday Mr. Flynn, a relation of the deceased, went again to Minver-place, where he saw Mrs. Manning. Mr. Flynn asked her if O'Connor had been there on the Thursday? She said he had not. According to the opinion of the witness, she appeared to be flurried and indisposed, and he asked her if she was ill. She said she had been ill a short time before, and that probably accounted for it. Early on the morning of the 13th, Manning went to a person named Bainbridge, a furniture broker, stated that he was going into the country for a time, and agreed to sell the whole of his furniture for £13. Manning required that the furniture should be removed the following morning at five o'clock, which was assented to, and Manning then agreed to lodge at Bainbridge's house for a fortnight. After the male prisoner had gone to Bainbridge's house, he sent a servant to his house in Minver-place for his wife. The servant returned, and said Mrs. Manning had been gone away an hour. Manning himself went to the house in Minver-place about five o'clock, and knocked at the door, but was not answered. He made inquiries, and was informed that his wife had left the house in a cab with some luggage. The broker's wife asked Manning the same day why, as the furniture was going to remain in the house that night, he did not sleep there, when he stated that he would not sleep in that house for twenty pounds. It appeared that, about four o'clock in the afternoon,

Mrs. Manning had packed up a large quantity of clothes and other articles; she called a cab from the stand, placed her boxes upon it with the assistance of the driver, and went to the South-Eastern Railway station, calling at a stationer's shop on the way, where she purchased some cards, and wrote upon them the address, "Mrs. Smith, passenger to Paris." On reaching the station she directed the porter to nail these cards on two of her boxes, which she left there. She then directed the driver to proceed to the Euston-square station; and, according to her own account, she went by railway to Newcastle, and was apprehended by the police on the 21st of of August, at Edinburgh, where she was passing under the name of Mrs. Smith. The police had reason to suspect she was Mrs. Manning. They charged her with it; she made no denial; she was asked for her keys, and gave them up. In her boxes, and upon her person, were found seventy-three sovereigns, a £50 note, a number of £10 notes—five of them being the notes obtained by the male prisoner at the Bank, a £5 note paid to Manning by the sharebroker, a quantity of Sambre and Meuse railway scrip, which was undoubtedly the property of O'Connor. He (the Attorney-General) had thus traced Mrs. Manning to the period of her apprehension, and he would now return to her husband. On the 15th of August, two days after the male prisoner had sold his furniture and taken lodgings at Bainbridge's, he hired a cab in the morning, and drove from Bermondsey-square to the Southampton Railway. He was followed, and on the 27th of August was apprehended at Jersey by the police officers. At this point of the case it was necessary that he (the Attorney-General) should do what would be afterwards done by their Lordships—caution the Jury against using adversely to the female prisoner any declarations made by the male prisoner upon his apprehension. It was necessary that the whole case should be detailed in evidence before the Jury, but the rules of law precluded the statements made by Manning from being used adversely against his wife. Manning, when he was apprehended, made no resistance; he said he was about to come to London to explain the whole matter; he stated in substance that the act was committed, not by himself, but by his wife, and that he was sure she would admit it in his presence and that of a clergyman; and he endeavoured, indeed, to cast the whole blame upon her. Manning described the manner in which the murder had been committed; he said his wife asked O'Connor to dinner, and that as he was going down-stairs she put her arm round his neck, and shot him in the head. Manning did not state, however, how it was that O'Connor's head had been so cruelly and frightfully mutilated—indeed, knocked to pieces—by some blunt instrument, probably the crow-bar. These were all the facts of the case. There could be no doubt whatever that the man O'Connor was murdered by somebody. The question for the Jury to determine was, whether both or either of the prisoners committed the act, or whether either of them did it with the knowledge and connivance of the other. They would find that, before the deed was committed, the lime which was undoubtedly used for the purpose of obliterating, if possible, all traces of the deceased, had been purchased by Manning, and delivered in the presence of his wife; that the crow-bar, which was well calculated to loosen the hard ground under which the unfortunate man was buried, and to raise the flag which it was hoped would cover him from observation, had been purchased by the male prisoner on the 23rd of July, delivered to the female prisoner on the 28th, and paid for by her; and that on the 8th of August the female prisoner herself purchased a shovel which, although it might be used for ordinary purposes, was handy and convenient for the removal of the earth. It was also evident that, without any notice, the prisoners quitted their house on the 13th of August, after repeated inquiries had been made there about O'Connor; and upon one of the prisoners was found a large amount of property, a great proportion of which was unquestionably the property of the deceased; while to the other was traced the possession of property of the deceased, which he (Manning) had converted into money in the name of O'Connor. These were the facts from which the Jury were to draw their conclusions. He (the Attorney-General) was sure they would do so calmly and fairly, patiently and honestly, dismissing from their minds all they had heard and read upon the subject, and relying solely upon what would be proved in evidence.

The first witness called was Henry Barnes, the policeman who discovered the remains of the unfortunate Patrick O'Connor.

HENRY BARNES'S EVIDENCE.

Henry Barnes, examined by Mr. Clarkson. He said: I am a police-constable of the K division. In consequence of information I had previously received, I went on Friday, the 17th of August last, to No. 3, Minver-place, accompanied by another officer named Burton, who had a key in his possession which unlocked the door. We found the house empty. In the back kitchen I observed a damp mark between the edges of two of the flag-stones, and this arrested my attention. With the assistance of Burton I removed the stones. There was mortar underneath, and then earth. The stones appeared to have been recently removed. We proceeded to remove portions of the earth, and when we had got about twelve inches down we came upon the toe of a man, and when about six inches further we came upon the loins of a man. The body was lying on the belly, and the legs were drawn back and tied to the haunches with a strong cord. The body was quite naked. We removed more earth, and at length we found the remainder of the body. The cord with which the legs were tied was about the size of a clothes' line. The body was completely imbedded in slacked lime. Mr. Lockwood, surgeon, came in during our operations, and, while the body remained lying in the hole, took a set of false teeth from the mouth. I did not examine the head closely, and did not see whether anything particular had happened to it. We removed the body into the front kitchen, where it was examined by Mr. Lockwood and Mr. Odling, another surgeon. Mr. Flynn came in also, and examined the body. The body remained in the house till after the inquest. On the same day I went to the residence of Mr. O'Connor, 21, Greenwood-street, Mile-end-road, where I saw a box said to belong to deceased. It was unlocked, but sealed. It had been forced open by Mr. Flynn on the 13th, and a seal afterwards put upon it. Within that box I found a cash-box, but no cash. There were only some I O U's, a few memoranda, and other papers.

By Mr. Sergeant Wilkins: One of the stones we removed from the floor of the back kitchen of No. 3, Minver-place, was about two feet square. The other was about three feet long and two feet wide. They were thick, heavy stones, and we were obliged to use a crow-bar to remove them. We borrowed a crow-bar for the purpose from some labourers. The soil we removed was wet, and was something like what is called "made earth." I am well acquainted with the premises now. There is a small garden at the back. Supposing one entered the house by the street-door, he would find the front parlour on the right-hand side of the passage. The two kitchens are under the parlours. There are houses on each side of it. I know nothing of the nature of the partitions, nor whether persons could be heard speaking in the adjoining houses.

James Burton, examined by Mr. Bodkin, said: I am a police-constable of the M division. On Tuesday, the 14th of August, I went to the house, No. 3, Minver-place, along with Mr. Keating, Mr. Meade, and another gentleman. We found it empty. I was there also on Friday, the 17th, when the stones were removed from the floor of the back kitchen, and the body found. The size of the opening was about 5 feet long, 2 feet broad, and between 2 and 3 feet deep.

By Mr. Sergeant Wilkins: I went to the house first, as I have said, on the 14th. On that occasion I found 28 pieces of linen, which appeared to be clean and fresh washed. I also found some boxes, but they were not such as goods are sent in. In the back kitchen I also found a shovel. Different shrubs were growing in the garden, and likewise some scarlet-runners, tied up with string.

MR. LOCKWOOD'S EVIDENCE.

Mr. Lockwood, examined by Mr. Clerk, said: I am a surgeon, residing in Newington. On the 17th August I went to the prisoners' house, No. 3, Minver-place, and found the constables Barnes and Burton there. I went into the back kitchen, and found that some slabs had been removed from the floor. Part of a body was visible in the hole from which the slabs had been removed. After some time I saw the body entirely uncovered. The legs were bent back to the haunches, and tied to the body in that position. Before the body was removed from the hole, I took from the mouth of the deceased a set of false teeth. The body was then taken to the front kitchen. Mr. Odling, another surgeon, cut the cords. I examined the head in the front kitchen. I perceived a protuberance, which was hard and moveable, over the right eye. I cut down upon it, and found a bullet inside, which I have now in my possession. [Mr. Lockwood here produced the bullet.] On the back part of the head I found extensive fractures. I could not trace the course of the bullet on account of the extensive fractures and the decomposition of the brain. I am not aware of the precise number of fractures, but I extracted sixteen pieces of bone. The wounds on the head were such as might have been produced by a crow-bar or chisel. There were contused as well as incised wounds. The fractures and the wound from the bullet would undoubtedly have occasioned death. I was present at the post mortem examination. The intestines of the deceased were perfectly healthy-looking; the brain was decomposed.

Mr. C. Slow, summoning officer, produced a set of false teeth, which he had received from Mr. Lockwood. Mr. Lockwood identified them as those he had taken from the body found at Minver-place.

Mr. W. Comley, dentist, 7, Osborne-street, Whitechapel, deposed that he knew the late Mr. O'Connor, and sold him the set of false teeth now produced.

Mr. Pierce Walshe, examined by the Attorney-General: I knew the deceased, Patrick O'Connor. On the 17th of August I went to the prisoners' house, but did not get in then. The next day I got in, and was shown a dead body, which I recognised as that of Patrick O'Connor. I saw him alive on the 8th of August, and was at his lodgings in Greenwood-street, Mile-end, and accompanied him thence to the house of the prisoners, in Minver-place. Mr. Manning let us in. It was about a quarter to ten o'clock. The male prisoner was at home, and we all sat down together. The female prisoner asked deceased why he did not come to dinner that day. She said they kept dinner waiting an hour, and wanted to know if he had got their dinner. The deceased said he had not. I said, perhaps she had posted it too late, and she remarked that no doubt he would get it the next day. The deceased then said that I was got the balance of Mr. Pitt's bill that day for him, and on which a prosecution had been taken out by the officers of the court at Charles-square, Hoxton. Mrs. Manning then asked the deceased if he would proceed against Pitt for the other three bills, and he said he would. There was nothing said about the other bills till Mrs. Manning made the remark. O'Connor and the male prisoner then began to smoke and converse together, and the former soon afterwards became faint, and sat upon the sofa, and some brandy and water was produced, but the deceased did not drink any. We went away about twelve o'clock. I accompanied the deceased on his way home, and when I left him he appeared quite well. I never saw him again alive. The prisoners appeared to be as friendly as brothers with the deceased.

By Mr. Ballantine: Mrs. Manning procured some eau-de-Cologne and bathed deceased's temples with it, but it did not appear to have the least effect in bringing him to.

By Mr Sergeant Wilkins: I believe Pitt is a grocer in the Bethnal-green-road.

Mr. W. Keating, examined by Mr. Bodkin, said: I am clerk in the Examiner's-office in the Customs. I knew the deceased. I saw him last alive on the evening of the 9th of August, on London-bridge, about a quarter to five. He was on the Surrey side of the bridge, and was going in that direction. A gentleman named Graham was with me, and we stopped and had some conversation with the deceased, and he shewed us a letter.

Mr. Bodkin: Did you notice the name?

Mr. Ballantine objected to the question, as he understood there was no evidence to shew that there was any connexion between the prisoners and that letter.

The Chief Baron admitted the objection.

Mr. Keating's examination continued: After some conversation with Mr. Graham and myself, deceased pursued his way towards Bermondsey, and he appeared in his usual health and spirits. On the Sunday following I went to Minver-place, and the female prisoner opened the door and let me in. I asked her if Mr. O'Connor had gone to dine there on the Thursday before, and she said he had not dined there on that day. I then asked her if she had not been at his lodgings on Thursday and Friday night, and she said she had; and she also told me that she went on the Thursday evening to inquire after his health, as he had been at her house the evening before, and was not well. I replied that it was very strange, as he had been seen on London-bridge by two friends going in that direction. She made no reply, and I asked if I could see Mr. Manning, as he might probably have seen him, and she told me that Mr. Manning thought it was very ungentlemanly of him not to keep his appointment to dinner. I thought she seemed very nervous while I was talking to her; and when I again inquired for Mr. Manning she said he was out, and she thought he was gone to church. I asked if I could see Mr. Manning in the evening, about six o'clock, if I called, and she told me they were both asked out to tea. I have frequently seen the female prisoner in company with Mr. O'Connor, and they appeared on very friendly terms. Manning and he also appeared to be on good terms.

By Mr. Ballantine: I never noticed any particular intimacy between Mrs. Manning and the deceased. I am aware that O'Connor and Mrs. Manning were acquainted with each other before Manning and he were acquainted. I have met Mrs. Manning and deceased walking together a good many times. When I have been at Mr. O'Connor's lodgings, I have also seen Mrs. Manning there. I have left them there alone as late as eight o'clock at night. Mrs. Manning told me she had been at O'Connor's lodgings on the 9th of August. She said she had been there about seven o'clock; but whether that was the time she left her own house or arrived at O'Connor's lodgings, I cannot say.

David Graham, examined by Mr. Clerk, said: I am an officer of the Customs. I was acquainted with the late Mr. O'Connor; and the last time I saw him alive was on the 9th of August, when Mr. Keating and I met him on London-bridge. It was about a quarter to five o'clock in the afternoon when we saw him. On the 12th of August I went with Mr. Keating to Minver-place. Mrs. Manning let us in. I saw no one else but Mrs. Manning. I recollect a conversation between Mr. Keating and Mrs. Manning. He asked when she had seen Mr. O'Connor, and she replied that she had not seen him since Wednesday, and he was then very unwell. He was obliged to lie down upon the sofa, and she rubbed his face with eau de Cologne. She also stated that she went to O'Connor's lodgings about seven o'clock on Thursday evening, for the purpose of ascertaining why he had not come to dinner. Mr. Manning, she said, thought it ungentlemanly of Mr. O'Connor not to come. Mr. Keating asked for Manning, and was told that he had gone to church. Mr. Keating said he would perhaps call and see him in the evening; but she said it would be of no use, as they were going out to tea.

By Mr. Sergeant Wilkins: Manning's house is about half a mile from the spot on London-bridge where I and Mr. Keating met O'Connor. They met him at a quarter before five o'clock.

By Mr. Parry: I knew Mr. O'Connor, but not very intimately. I have seen Mrs. Manning and him walking together three or four times. I also saw Mrs. Manning once at O'Connor's house. I left them together, and they appeared very friendly. Mr. O'Connor occupied two rooms on one floor—a bed-room and sitting-room.

It being now nearly two o'clock, the Court and Jury adjourned a few minutes for the purpose of taking some refreshment. Upon their return,

Mr. James Coleman, examined by the Attorney-General, said: I am a broker in the Customs. I knew the late Mr. O'Connor for eight or ten years. I saw him last on the 9th of August, in Weston-street, about 150 yards from Minver-place. It was about ten minutes after five when I saw him.

By Mr. Sergeant Wilkins: He was going in the direction of Minver-place.

John Younghusband, examined by the Attorney-General, said: He knew the late Mr. O'Connor. He saw him last on the 9th of August, on London-bridge. It was about a quarter-past five o'clock when he saw him. He was walking very slowly, and stopping, as it undecided which way to go. Witness was on the top of an omnibus.

By Mr. Sergeant Wilkins: O'Connor was walking towards the City at the moment witness saw him.

Sophia Payne, examined by Mr. Clarkson, said: I live at 2, Minver-place. I know Manning, the male prisoner. I remember hearing a rumour of the murder of Mr. O'Connor. On the Monday after I heard it Manning came to my door, about six o'clock in the evening, and asked permission to go through my house to his own, because his wife had gone out. I gave him permission, and he got over the garden-wall to his own house. On the Thursday before that Monday, I saw him, about a quarter to seven in the evening, sitting on his garden-wall, smoking a pipe. I conversed with him about 20 minutes, when he suddenly jumped down, saying he had an appointment to attend to which he had forgotten, and he must go and dress. I saw him no more that evening. I left home about half-past seven, and returned about eleven. I left my husband at home.

By Mr. Sergeant Wilkins: It was quite light when I saw the prisoner Manning on the garden-wall. He was sitting with his legs towards his own garden. He was dressed as usual, and looked as usual. His garden was rather larger than ours. He had flowers in it; but I am not aware whether he was in the habit of paying particular attention to them. When people are bustling about in the house adjoining ours, we can hear them, if we are quiet. We take tea about five o'clock. During that time we are rather quiet. Lithograph printing is carried on in our house; but it does not commence till seven in the evening. There is nothing else in our house likely to make a noise.

By Mr. Clarkson: I have children; but I always keep them very quiet.

By the Attorney-General: I am quite sure about the hour at which I had the conversation with the male prisoner, Manning, in the garden; for it was just before my husband came home. He generally comes home at seven o'clock.

Mr. Flynn, examined by Mr. Bodkin, said: I am an officer of the Customs. I was acquainted with the deceased, Mr. O'Connor. In consequence of his absence from home, I went to Minver-place on Sunday, the 12th of August, to make inquiries about him, but I did not get in. I went again on Monday, accompanied by a police-officer, in private clothes. I saw Mrs. Manning, and had some conversation with her. I asked for her husband, and she said he was not in. I said I was a friend of Mr. O'Connor's, and wanted to know if she or her husband had heard anything of him? She said "No." I said it was very strange; and she replied, that it was very odd indeed, for some friends had seen him on London-bridge on the 9th. She mentioned Mr. Keating's name as one of the persons who had seen him. She said that Mr. O'Connor was a very fickle-minded man; he often came into her house, and stopped a minute or two, and then suddenly jumped up and went away. She then said it was probable he was at a place at Vauxhall, where she had been with him once or twice, and she mentioned the name of Walshe. After this she said, "Poor Mr. O'Connor; he was the best friend I had in London." When she said this, I fancied her countenance changed, and she became pale; and I inquired if she was ill, or if the room was too warm? She replied, "No;" and that six weeks before she had been ill. I next asked her if she had been to Mr. O'Connor's lodgings on the 9th; and she said she had. I asked her what time she left her own place, and she at first said six o'clock; and on my asking if she was certain of the time, she said it might be a quarter-past; and she added, that she had met one or two friends going down. As I was leaving her she said, "You gentlemen are very susceptible."

Mr. Bodkin: Did she give any explanation of this expression?

Witness: She did not.

By Mr. Sergeant Wilkins: The deceased kept his money in [a cash-box in his trunk, and his trunk stood in his bed-room.

By the Attorney-General: I went to the lodgings of the deceased after I had been at Minver-place. I forced open his trunk, and found in his cash-box a few memoranda, but no money.

By a Juryman: There was nothing said by me to elicit from Mrs. Manning the expression, "Poor Mr. O'Connor."

Ann Armes, residing in Greenwood-street, Mile-end-road, was next called: Mr. O'Connor resided in my house nearly five years. He occupied two rooms on the first floor, ready furnished. I recollect that he left my house on the morning of the 9th of August, at half-past seven o'clock. There are two doors to my house—one to the shop, and one to Mr. O'Connor's rooms. He never returned after going out on the day I have mentioned. I know the female prisoner. She was in the habit of visiting Mr. O'Connor, particularly during the last month before he disappeared. She generally came alone; but once or twice Mr. Manning came with her, and also Mr. Massey. I saw Mrs. Manning go up-stairs to Mr. O'Connor's rooms at a quarter-past six o'clock on the evening of the 9th of August. She remained till a quarter-past seven o'clock. No one else called that evening. On leaving the house, Mrs. Manning came through the shop. She usually went out by the private door. I saw her again next day, when she came about the same time, and went up-stairs to Mr. O'Connor's room. She remained till a quarter past seven o'clock; and, on passing through the shop, she changed half-a-crown, and bought some article. I thought there was something singular about her appearance. She trembled very much. I noticed that she gave the money with her left hand. On Friday, Mr. Flynn came to O'Connor's lodgings. On the Friday before Mr. O'Connor left, Mrs. Manning came alone, and went into Mr. O'Connor's room. I heard Mrs. Manning then say she wanted to purchase some railway shares. Mr. O'Connor had his cash-box before him, and had taken out some papers, which lay on the table.

Cross-examined by Mr. Sergeant Wilkins: Mr. O'Connor always carried his keys on his own person. When Mrs. Manning came she usually had tea with Mr. O'Connor. The key of the tea-caddy, from which Mr. O'Connor took the tea, was on the bunch, among his other keys. I have seen Mr. Manning along with Mrs. Manning, at Mr. O'Connor's lodgings; Mr. Massey also. They all seemed on good terms. My parlour is under Mr. O'Connor's room. During business hours, I am sometimes in the shop, and sometimes in the parlour; and I can hear any one passing up. When Mrs. Manning paid the money with her left hand, she seemed to have a parcel in her right. On the Friday evening, previous to Mr. O'Connor's going, I saw the cash-box lying on the table in Mrs. Manning's presence. I have seen Mrs. Manning in O'Connor's bed-room, but never when they were alone.

By Mr. Ballantine: Did not hear Mrs. Manning say where she had got her money to buy shares. When the cash-box was on the table, O'Connor seemed to be pointing out certain papers to Mrs. Manning. He pointed to particular papers, and said, "These would be the best." O'Connor had lodged with me about five years, and the Mannings had visited him for about twelve months. Mrs. Manning never slept in the house, to my knowledge. I never was paid any sum for her by O'Connor. I never was paid nine shillings on her account by O'Connor. Some boxes once came, with the name of Roux on them; but they were not allowed to go up-stairs. I think Mrs. Manning came at the same time with the boxes. This was about a year and three months ago.

Emily Armes, examined by Mr. Clerk. Is sister to the preceding witness. Recollects the time when Mr. O'Connor was missing. On the Friday previous, heard a conversation between Mr. O'Connor and Mrs. Manning. It was about railway shares. She said she wished to buy some. O'Connor was showing her some shares, and he said, pointing to a lot, "No, not that." He then advised her to purchase some shares, the name of which I forget. On the Thursday evening after Mr. O'Connor went away, Mrs. Manning came and asked if he was at home? She was told he was not, and she then passed on to his room. I observed her looking very pale when she went out, as she was purchasing some biscuits in the shop. Next night (Friday) she again called, and went up-stairs into his room as before. She this night also, looked very pale and shaky as she passed out. There was a difference in her appearance on Friday as compared with Thursday. She was more shaky, and her left hand trembled very much.

By Mr. Sergeant Wilkins: Mrs. Manning was paler than usual. She bought some cake on Thursday, and paid for it with coppers. She was dressed in a visite. When she asked for O'Connor, the witness did not say that he had been out all night.

By Mr. Ballantine: Mrs. Manning, on going out, could have passed through the private door, and not come near the shop at all. On previous occasions she had done so, when Mr. O'Connor let her out. I have also let her out by the private door. I am not a servant in the house, but live with my sister. I recollect some boxes coming, with the address, "Miss Rouf" upon them. It was not "Roux;" I am certain of that. Mrs. Manning came with the boxes. She had a bed at our house that night. Mr. O'Connor asked whether we could provide a bed for his friend and her husband. The husband did not come.

By the Attorney-General: I have seen the letter now produced. It was brought to our house on Friday, the 10th, by a person who said he was from the Docks. I believe the writing inside to be that of the female prisoner.

By Mr. Ballantine: Mr. O'Connor never paid 9s. on account of Mrs. Manning having slept in the house.

WILLIAM MASSEY'S EVIDENCE.

William Massey, medical student, was examined by the Attorney-General: I resided with the Mannings for fourteen weeks. They kept no servant, but a charwoman was occasionally employed. I left on the 28th of July, because they appeared anxious that I should do so. They said they were going out of town on Monday, and I left on the Saturday. I have frequently seen Mr. O'Connor there. The male prisoner has sometimes spoken to me about him. He once told me his wife had been to the Docks, where she had seen O'Connor in a state of intoxication, he having taken large quantities of brandy as a precaution against cholera. He told me also that she had seen his will, and that he had left her all, or the greatest part of his property, and that he was a man worth £20,000.

The Attorney-General: Has he on those occasions ever spoken to you of drugs that will produce stupefaction?—He has—he has spoken of laudanum. In the first place, he asked me what would best produce stupefaction, or partial intoxication, so as to get a person to put his hand to paper. He asked whether chloroform or laudanum would produce stupefaction. I said these drugs had no doubt been used for such purposes. When speaking of these things he had just before mentioned the name of O'Connor, and had referred to his having a considerable amount of money. He said O'Connor was very apprehensive of cholera; and he observed to me, "You frighten him well about the cholera, and persuade him to take brandy as a specific for it."

Did he ever ask you any questions about the head?—Yes; he once asked me what part of the head it would be most fatal to strike. I said I believed that a blow behind the ear would most likely be attended with fatal effects. He once asked me where the brain was placed, and I pointed out the part.

Was there anything said about an air-gun?—There was. He asked me about the nature of an air-gun, and I said I had heard of such a thing, but that I had never fired one.

Did you ever talk about what would be the fate of a murderer?—We once talked on that subject. Something was said about the wax figure of Rush at Madame Tussaud's, and he asked me if a murderer went to heaven. I said "No."

Have you ever written letters for this man?—I have written a letter or two, at his request, to Mr. O'Connor.

By Mr. Sergeant Wilkins: You being a medical student, questions connected with your profession sometimes became the topic of conversation?—Yes.

Mary Wells: My father carries on the business of a builder. I know the male prisoner, and remember him coming to my father's house to purchase lime some time at the end of July. He said he wanted it to kill slugs in the garden. I asked him which he would have, white or grey. He said he would have that kind which burned quickest. We had no white, and he then said he would take grey, and he wrote a direction on paper where to send it to. I delivered that direction to Richard Welsh, who was the person sent with the lime.

By Mr. Sergeant Wilkins: Our house is five minutes' walk from Minver-place. The servant was present at the time, and might hear all that passed. The lime was sent home two days afterwards, and no inquiry was made after it in the meantime.

Richard Welsh, a boy in the employment of Mr. Wells, was next called: I carried some lime to Minver-place, on the 25th of July. I saw the prisoner Manning order the lime. When I took it to Minver-place I saw the female prisoner. There was a bushel of lime. I took it down to the kitchen by direction of Mr. Manning, where I shot it into a basket. Mr. Manning asked me to call next day, and he would see if he could get a couple of halfpennies for me. I called next day, and got three-halfpence from Mrs. Manning.

By Mr. Sergeant Wilkins: I was present when the lime was ordered. The direction was given to me, but I did not read it. I had heard Manning give his address as well as write it; and I knew where to go.

William Danby, examined by Mr. Bodkin: I am in the employment of Mr. Evans, an ironmonger in King William-street. On the 25th of July the male prisoner ordered a crow-bar, in all respects the same as that now produced, except that it was five inches longer. He directed it to be sent to No. 3, Minver-place. I took it home on the 28th July. The prisoner was told the price would be 2s. 6d. As I was going along, carrying the crow-bar in my hand, the male prisoner met me on the bridge, and asked if I had a crow-bar for him? He said I ought to have wrapped it up in paper, as he did not wish everybody to see what he was purchasing. He then went into a stationer's shop and bought some brown paper, which he put round the crow-bar and tied it with a string. He then went to the corner of the Maze, and showed me the way to his house, saying that some one there would pay for the crow-bar. A stout lady (Mrs. Manning) opened the door to me. The crow-bar was at this time so covered up that no part of it could be seen. Mrs. Manning asked if I had brought that from King William-street. I said "Yes," and gave her the bill, when she complained that it was charged rather more than was agreed for at the shop. I got 6s. 6d. for it.

By Mr. Sergeant Wilkins: There were three or four persons in the shop when the crow-bar was ordered. If Manning had not given his address, I should not have known where to take it to, as I never saw him before. On going to the stationer's shop, he said we might have wrapped it up in paper; but he did not say that any respectable dealer would have done so.

By Mr. Ballantine: When Mr. Manning ordered the crow-bar, he did not say what he wanted it for. I do not know whether it was termed a "chisel," a "ripping chisel," or a "crow-bar," in the bill. There was more than one fold of paper over it when I took it to Minver-place. When Manning left me, we were not more than five minutes' walk from his house.

Mr. Lockwood, the surgeon, was recalled; and, in answer to questions put by the Attorney-General, said that, in his opinion, such an instrument as that now produced, or one five or six inches longer, would inflict the wounds he saw on the head of Mr. O'Connor.

By Mr. Sergeant Wilkins: The wounds might have been inflicted by a shorter as well as by a longer instrument than that now produced.

By the Chief Baron: You stated in your evidence that some of the wounds were incised and some of them contused?—Yes.

Could you, from the appearance of the wounds, form any opinion as to the length of time which had elapsed since they were inflicted?—I could not; but I think they were inflicted

inflicted a week or so before. I have no doubt that when I saw the body it must have been under the ground a week at least.

What grounds have you for thinking so?—The body was in such a state of extensive decomposition as led me to think so.

In forming your judgment, did you take into consideration the fact that lime had been used?—I did. The lime would certainly cause the body to decompose quicker.

By the Chief Baron: Taking into consideration the quantity of lime used, can you still form an opinion as to whether the body had been under the ground for a week or less?—I have no doubt whatever that it was there for a week.

By Mr. Sergeant Wilkins: Did you arrive at this conclusion from what you had previously heard?—I formed my opinion upon the matter the very day the body was taken out of the ground.

Had you previously heard that the body was missing?—I had heard that, but I formed my judgment entirely from the appearance of the body.

By the Jury: Would not the effect of the lime be to disfigure the features very much?—Yes; and a stranger might not be able to trace them.

By the Chief Baron: Were the features so destroyed as to render it difficult to identify the body?—Probably a person intimately acquainted with the person of the deceased would be able to identify him.

Would the external application of lime make any difference with respect to the decomposition of the brain, which I understood you to say was found in a fluid state?—The lime might be absorbed through the fractures of the skull, and so cause the decomposition of the brain.

Did you examine the intestines, and did their appearance throw any light upon the time which the body had lain under ground?—I did, along with Mr. Odling; and they were found as much decomposed as the other appearances would have led me to expect.

William Cahill, examined by Mr. Clerk: I am shopman to Mr. Langley, an ironmonger in Tooley-street. On the 8th of August the female prisoner came to the shop to purchase a shovel, and she said she wished to have a strong one. I recommended her to have a regular wooden-handled long one, but she said a short one would do, and she purchased one; and I took it to the address she gave me—No. 3, Minver-place. The shovel produced is the one I sold her.

By Mr. Ballantine: This shovel cost 1s. 3d. She might have purchased a common spade for 2s.

William Sopp proved that he obtained the shovel referred to by the last witness from Mr. Bainbridge, the broker, to whom the prisoners had sold all their furniture.

Henry Barnes, the police constable, recalled: I am sure the shovel was not in the house on the day when I found the body.

By Mr. Sergeant Wilkins: I went into the front parlour and saw a new marble chimney-piece there, but did not observe that there was any want of paper round the top of it.

Hannah Firman, examined by the Attorney-General: I am twelve years old. On Friday, the 10th of August, I was in Minver-place, selling matches and shoe-ties, when I saw a woman, and I asked her if she wanted her steps cleaned. She said to me, "Can you come on Monday?" and I told her I could not. She then asked me if I could do anything else besides cleaning steps, and I told her I could, and I offered to do some work for her for 5d. I offered to clean the back kitchen, but she told me she had done that herself, and she then wanted me to wash a basket with marks of lime on it. I told her I could not do so, because my hand was bad, and the prisoner then let the water run through the basket until it all ran away.

Do you see that woman here?—The witness looked round the whole court before she turned towards the dock, and, immediately on her eyes resting on Mrs. Manning, she exclaimed, "There she is." I heard a conversation between Mr. Manning and his wife. I was at the coal-cellar when I heard the male prisoner stamp with his foot, and say to his wife, "Give it me directly." She replied that she would, and I heard no more, as I was then in the coal-hole.

By Mr. Ballantine: The kitchen looked neither very clean nor very dirty. They gave me 8d. for my work, but I was not scolded into the bargain.

Now, tell me, did you take anything away with you from the house?—The witness here showed some hesitation, but on Mr. Ballantine repeating the question, she exclaimed, "Yes, sir; I will tell the truth, for it will go furthest."

That's right. Now, tell us what you did take away?—I cannot tell everything. I took an egg from the larder.

And a razor?—Yes, sir.

Where from?—From a box.

You took an egg from the larder and a razor from the box. Was there anything more?—Yes, sir, a purse out of the drawer.

Anything besides the purse?—I do not remember.

Did you not take some stockings—two pairs of stockings?—No, sir; not two pairs, I only took one pair out of the cupboard.

Then you took some clothes belonging to Mrs. Manning—a dress and petticoat, did you not?—I don't recollect any more, sir.

Nor a smelling-bottle?—I don't remember about the smelling-bottle.

Mr. Ballantine: Oh! you can't recollect any more. You may go.

The witness then left the court, having, by the confession of these various thefts, left an impression on the minds of the audience very different from that which she had created during the first part of her evidence, which she gave with much clearness and appearance of simplicity.

James Coleman, a builder, and landlord of No 3, Minver-place, proved that he let the house to the Mannings, and that they left it without notice, though they were yearly tenants. On the Tuesday evening succeeding the 9th of August, he found the house empty.

By Mr. Sergeant Wilkins: No marble chimney-piece was put up by the Mannings.

MR. BAINBRIDGE'S EVIDENCE.

Charles Bainbridge said: I am a broker in Bermondsey-square. I had known the male prisoner for about two months before July last. He made me an offer to sell his furniture, and I went over the house with the female prisoner, and agreed to give her £13 for the whole of it. Mrs. Manning wanted £16, and I refused to give it; and on the 13th of August I agreed to give £13 10s. The male prisoner wanted me to take the furniture on the following morning, at five o'clock, but I refused, saying it would look bad. The male prisoner afterwards told me that his "governor" was not going away for a fortnight, and he proposed to lodge with me for that time; and he agreed to give 10s. per week. Shortly after this he told me that he had started his wife off into the country, and that night he slept at my house. There was some linen in the house which was not included in my purchase, and he wished me to take charge of it, and also a new hat; and he said he should be in the country about two months. Among the property which I removed from the prisoner's house, was the new shovel which has been produced. I last saw the male prisoner on the morning of the 15th of August.

By Mr. Sergeant Wilkins: I am sure the prisoner said that he had started his wife off into the country. He slept at my house on the Monday night and the Tuesday night, and he went away on the following morning. There was no coalpick or axe among the articles I purchased of the prisoner.

By Mr. Bodkin: There was no crow-bar among the articles.

Mrs. Bainbridge, the wife of the last witness, deposed that, upon examining a dress, which was one of the articles purchased by her husband, she observed a mark as though there had been blood upon it, and it appeared to her as though it had been imperfectly washed and dried, and had become mildewed. The male prisoner left their house on the Wednesday morning, taking with him a carpet-bag and a trunk, and he told her he was going to sea-bathing. On the Monday before he went away he told her that he had sent his wife off into the country. At this time the goods were still in the house in Minver-place, and she asked the prisoner whether he would sleep there, and he said, "I would not sleep there for £20."

By Mr. Sergeant Wilkins: Witness would swear the prisoner did not say that his wife had started off into the country, but that he had sent her there himself.

The witness was cross-examined at some length as to her reason for supposing that there were marks of blood upon the dress, but she only repeated that the dress appeared to her to have been washed and imperfectly dried. The spots of blood, she thought, would not come out without boiling.

Matilda Wellden deposed that in August last she was living at Mr. Bainbridge's as servant, and remembered the prisoner Fredrick Manning coming there on the 13th of August. He sent her to Minver-place to fetch his wife, but she could not find the house, and the prisoner then went himself. On the evening before the goods were removed, he told her that if anybody inquired for him, she was to say that she had not seen him for a fortnight.

By Mr. Sergeant Wilkins: When she was first examined, she said she did not know whether the prisoner said that his wife had gone into the country, or whether he had sent her there.

Mrs. Scholefield deposed that she lived opposite the prisoners' house in Minver-place. About half-past 3 o'clock on Monday, the 13th of August, she saw the female prisoner go away in a cab, with several boxes and other luggage. The male prisoner went to the house about half-past 5, and knocked at the door and the window, and when he found he could not get in, he came to her and asked if she had seen his wife go away. She told him she had; and he then asked if she had any luggage with her, and she said she had. The prisoner then thanked her and went over to Minver-place, and knocked at No. 2, and went in.

William Byford, the driver of a hackney-cab, deposed that he drove the male prisoner to the Southampton Railway station on the morning of the 14th of August, and by his direction he went through Bermondsey-street, which was much further round.

William Kirk, cab-driver, said: On the 13th of August, the female prisoner came to the stand where I was, and hired my cab. It was about half-past three o'clock. She asked me to take two boxes and other things from the house in Minver-place to the cab. She got out on the hill, coming to London-bridge, and went in to a stationer's. I then drove to the

London-bridge station, and there saw some cards attached to the boxes. She left two boxes there, and I then drove her to the Euston station.

W. Day, porter at the London-bridge terminus: On the 16th of August I recollect the female prisoner leaving two boxes at the station. She gave me two cards, on which were written either "Mrs." or "Miss Smith, passenger, Paris." I placed them on the boxes, and took the latter to the cloak-room, to be left till called for.

MR. RICHARD J. MOXHAY'S EVIDENCE.

Richard J. Moxhay, superintendent of police, Edinburgh: On the 21st of August, I went with a Mr. Dobson to a lodging-house in Leith-walk. I left Mr. Dobson at the door, and, going into a room, saw a lady. I said, "Mrs. Smith, I presume?" and then I added, "May I be allowed to ask if you are a married lady?" She said she was, and that her husband's name had been Smith, but that he was dead. She stated that she came to town on the Tuesday or Wednesday previously, and that there was no person in Edinburgh to whom she could refer but Mr. Shaw, a gentleman over the way, who had recommended her to the lodgings in which I found her. She further stated that she had last come from Newcastle, and that her object was to improve her health, adding that she had bathed at Portobello. I asked if she had any scrip? when she said, "What do you mean by scrip?" I replied, "Any railway shares?" when she said she had not, nor had she been offering any for sale, I then looked very intently at her, and said, "My impression is that you are the wife of Frederick George Manning." I then directed an officer who accompanied me to ask Mr. Dobson to come in. That gentleman accordingly entered, and said, "That is the lady who offered me scrip for sale." I asked her if she had any objection to let me see her luggage, and she said, "Certainly not." I got her keys from her, and, on opening a trunk, the first thing found was a tavern bill-head, with the name "F. G. Manning, Taunton," upon it. The moment I saw that, I said, "My suspicions are confirmed; put all these things up;" and then turning to Mrs. Manning, I informed her that I was the superintendent of police, and, after cautioning her in the usual terms, I asked if she had any scrip? She replied—"Scrip? Oh yes, scrip of my own." She said she had no objection to my looking at it. In one of her trunks I found a certain number of sovereigns, and scrip of the Sambre and Meuse Railway, numbered from 6460 to 6469 inclusive, and also of the same railway, numbered from 26,523 to 26,532 both inclusive. There was also scrip of the Boulogne and Amiens Railway, numbered from 48,865 to 48,874, both inclusive; a certificate of Spanish bonds, numbered 3620, and some other scrip. There was a purse containing 73 sovereigns; also a Bank of England note for £50, numbered 11,087, and dated the 9th of November, 1848; six £10 Bank of England notes, five of which were numbered from 67,372 to 67,376, and the remaining one 78,378; and one Bank of England note was numbered 20,051. There was, besides, a luggage-ticket; and a ticket for excess of luggage between London and Newcastle, having upon it the name of Smith, and a number of other articles. I asked her about her husband after taking her to the police-office. I asked her if she had any objection to tell me where he was? She said, "Upon my honour, I do not know. I came off from London suddenly, when he was out, on Monday afternoon. I took a cab and drove with my luggage to the London-bridge terminus of the Brighton Railway. I there left part of my luggage, on which I put the address, 'Mrs. Smith, passenger for France,' and then drove to the Euston station." She alluded to O'Connor, and said, "Murder O'Connor! Certainly not; he was the kindest friend I ever had in the world! he acted the part of a father to me. I last saw him on Wednesday night. He came the worse for liquor, and went away late. We expected him on Thursday to dinner, but he did not come; and, as I was rather surprised at it, I went to his house to inquire for him." She then stated that when Friday came, he not making his appearance, she again went to ask after him, but could get no account of him. She made reference to her husband, and complained of his bad usage of her. She said he maltreated her, and once pursued her with a knife, and threatened to cut off her head. One of their chief causes of quarrel was that he could not get the money she had.

By Mr. Sergeant Wilkins: Mrs. Manning stated that when she first started from home she did not know, up to that moment, whether to go to Paris or to Scotland.

By Mr. Ballantine: She said that part of the scrip found in her possession had been purchased for her by Mr. O'Connor.

MR. EDWARD LANGLEY'S EVIDENCE.

Edward Langley, sergeant of police, deposed: I went to Jersey on the 25th of August, and reached Prospect-house on the 27th. When I, accompanied by several other persons, went into the room where Manning was, the latter exclaimed, "Holloa, what are you all about?" I made myself known to the prisoner, who then said, "Is that you, sergeant? I am glad you are come. I was going to London to explain it all." He then said, "Is the wretch taken?" I said, "I do not know." He said, "I suppose they will find a great deal of money upon her—£1800 or £1400 at least." I said I did not know, and that he must consider himself in custody for the shocking affair that had taken place in his house. His reply was, "Very well—I can explain it all; but surely you will not put the handcuffs on me." The prisoner was then taken down-stairs. On going along he said, "She shot him; the cloth was laid on the table, and she asked him to go down-stairs and wash his hands. At the bottom of the stairs she put one hand on his shoulder, and with the other shot him in the back of the head." Captain Chevalier, who was one of the party, asked what had become of the body, and he said, "She had a grave dug for him." No other questions were put to him. On the following morning the prisoner asked how long he would be kept, as he was anxious to go to London to explain everything. He was brought to Southampton in the packet, and on our arrival there I met Inspector Haynes, who accompanied us to town. During the journey from Southampton, he asked whether, if his wife confessed, he would be set free. I said he must excuse me from answering such a question. He said, "I am sure she will confess, when she sees me, particularly if a clergyman is present." I examined his clothes, and in one of the pockets I found some tissue paper and some gunpowder. The prisoner seemed very unwell. In the railway carriage he began talking to Inspector Haynes, but I, being very tired fell asleep.

MR. J. HAYNES'S EVIDENCE.

J. Haynes, superintendent of the detective police, said: In consequence of information I received, I went to London-bridge station, and found two boxes, with a direction on each. The address was "Mrs. Smith, passenger to Paris; to lie till called for." I opened one of those boxes, and found several articles. There were marks of blood on the skirt of a gown, which appeared to have been recently washed. I found a piece of muslin also similarly stained. Was at Southampton on the 31st of August, and came up in the train with the male prisoner. He asked me if I had seen his wife? I said I had not. He said, "Do you think I shall see her to-morrow?" I replied, "I don't know; but I don't think it is likely you will be allowed to see her." I had previously said, "This is a very serious affair, Manning, but you are not required to say anything to criminate yourself." He said, "I am aware of that. I was very foolish to go away, for I ought to have staid and explained all." He said if he could see his wife in the presence of a clergyman, he was sure she would explain all, for it was she who shot O'Connor. She invited him to dinner, and had laid the cloth, and then shot him from behind when going down-stairs. He said she was a very violent woman, and would think no more of killing a man than of killing a cat—that he had been frequently afraid of his own life, and that on one occasion she followed him with a drawn knife. He said that she was determined to be revenged on O'Connor, for he it was who had induced them to take the house in Minver-place. He said it cost them £30 to furnish the house, and O'Connor had promised to come and lodge with them; that he was out of town at the time, and that, on his return, his wife told him O'Connor had only slept there one night, and refused to remain longer. When he said his wife shot him, I observed that it appeared by the papers there were other wounds on the head, but he made no reply to that.

The Attorney-General then put in as evidence the letter referred to by him in his opening statement, written by Mrs. Manning to O'Connor, containing an invitation to dinner, and which was found open at O'Connor's lodgings on the Thursday.

The Court adjourned, at a little after 6 o'clock, till 10 next morning.

The prisoners left the dock without taking the slightest notice of each other. Mrs. Manning, before leaving, curtsied slightly towards the Bench, and was led out by a female turnkey.

SECOND DAY.—FRIDAY, OCTOBER 26.

The trial was resumed at ten o'clock, when Lord Chief Baron Pollock and Mr. Justice Cresswell took their seats on the bench in the morning. Mr. Justice Maule was absent.

John Haines, who was the last witness examined, and who then produced some dresses and a piece of muslin found in the boxes left by Mrs. Manning at the South-Eastern Railway station at London bridge, was recalled, and stated that he delivered to Mr. William Odling one of those dresses and the muslin collar.

Mr. William Odling, examined by Mr. Bodkin: I am a practising chemist. I have examined a part of this dress, which I have subjected to the usual chemical test; and I have arrived at the conclusion that the stains upon it were caused by blood.

Cross-examined by Mr. Ballantine: The tests were applied on Wednesday last. I was not examined before the police-magistrates. No person but myself was present when I applied the tests. I am twenty years old. I allowed the dress to stand in cold distilled water. I cannot say that the stain on the collar is blood.

Re-examined by Mr. Bodkin: I am a son of Mr. Odling, surgeon to the police force. I have been studying chemistry for five years at least. I have studied at Guy's Hospital and at the College of Chemistry. There was very little of stain on the collar, compared with what was on the dress. The stain was not iron-mould; nor any vegetable matter which I am acquainted with.

In answer to questions put by the Lord Chief Baron, the witness described the usual negative chemical tests to which presumed blood-stains are subjected, and which he had applied in the present instance, adding that there was no direct chemical process by which the presence of blood-stains could be ascertained.

MR. FRANCIS WORRALL STEPHENS'S EVIDENCE.

Francis Worrall Stephens, examined by Mr. Clarkson: I am a stockbroker, carrying on business at No. 3, Royal Exchange. I was acquainted with the late Patrick O'Connor. I was in the habit of doing business with him. I delivered to him, on the 6th of August last, ten shares in the Sambre and Meuse Railway. I had purchased them for him on the 3rd of August. They were numbered 6460 to 6469 inclusive. I think they were ordered on the 2nd or 3rd of August. In May last I purchased for O'Connor ten shares in the Amiens and Boulogne Railway. They were ordered on or before the 11th of May. I delivered them on the 11th. They were numbered 48,665 to 48,674 inclusive. I recollect Mrs. Manning coming to my office either on the 1st, 2nd, or 3rd of August—but I rather think it was the 1st. She introduced herself by saying that she had been recommended to me by Patrick O'Connor, as she wanted to invest some money. She asked what shares or stock she could buy in England that she could sell abroad. I asked where she was going to. After some hesitation, she said to Paris. I said, "Perhaps you had better purchase French Rentes?" She asked for the Foreign Railway List, and I showed it to her. She asked what shares she should buy, as she wished to sell the property again without the control of her husband? She asked, if she purchased Boulogne and Amiens shares, or Sambre and Meuse, whether she could sell them without her husband's control? She said she would call again, and went away; but I did not see her afterwards.

Cross-examined by Mr. Ballantine: The Boulogne and Amiens shares came to £71 17s. 6d. They have diminished in value since I bought them for O'Connor. In August they would have been worth about £7 per share. O'Connor never mentioned Mrs. Manning's name to me.

MR. ALEXANDER LAMOND'S EVIDENCE.

Alexander Lamond, examined by Mr. Clerk: I am not a broker on the Stock Exchange, but I am a stockbroker. I was acquainted with O'Connor when he was alive. In April last I purchased some shares in the Eastern Counties Railway for him. I witnessed the transfer of those shares to Mr. Patrick O'Connor. They were twenty shares, and amounted to £400 of the Consolidated Stock of the Eastern Counties Railway. [The transfer-book of the railway company was here produced, from which it appeared that the transfer was executed on the 16th May last.] The shares were paid for on the same day. On the 27th of April, I purchased for O'Connor ten shares in the Sambre and Meuse Railway. They are scrip shares, which pass from hand to hand without registration. I do not know the numbers of those shares. I received them from Mr. George Cooper Russell. Russell's name was on them. [Mr. Moxhay, the superintendent of police at Edinburgh, here produced the Sambre and Meuse scrip found in Mrs. Manning's trunk.] I recognise these as the shares which passed through our hands with reference to that transaction. These shares were brought to our office by Mr. Wenham Russell's clerk. They are numbered 26,523 to 26,532 inclusive.

Cross-examined by Mr. Ballantine: Mrs. Manning brought me a note of introduction from O'Connor. She asked me some questions, but she had no dealings with me.

John Hayward, examined by the Attorney-General: I am a clerk in the office of the solicitor to the Treasury. I was present at the police-office when a person named John Bassett was examined. I understand that he is now dead. He produced before the magistrate, and I received from him, this scrip and assignment [producing them]. They have been in my possession ever since.

Mr. Green examined: I am clerk of the transfers to the Eastern Counties Railway Company. This is the original certificate of Eastern Counties Railway Company's shares delivered to Patrick O'Connor. The other document professes to be an assignment of those shares.

Mr. Shillibeer examined: I know Frederick George Manning. I do not believe that the signature to this document (the assignment) is in his handwriting. It does not bear the slightest resemblance to it. [This unexpected statement from the witness excited a good deal of surprise.]

Richard Hammond, examined by the Attorney-General: I am a clerk in the employment of Messrs. Killick and Co., sharebrokers. I know the male prisoner. I did not see him execute this transfer of stock, but it was brought to me wet by Mr. Bassett. At the time when Bassett brought it to me I saw the male prisoner in the office. When he came in, we spoke about Eastern Counties shares, and I introduced him to Mr. Bassett in the private room. He said he had been there before, but I did not know what his name was. Mr. Bassett asked me for £110, and I gave him the money. I gave him a £100 Bank of England note, numbered 15,043, and dated the 5th of June, 1849. There was also a £5 note, numbered 20,051, and five sovereigns. I saw him pay this money to the prisoner, Frederick George Manning. The words "Patrick O'Connor" on the assignment were wet when it was delivered to me, and I put it on the blotting-paper. There was a Mr. Lintorn, a share-dealer, who was in the office at the time. I did not hear the name of O'Connor mentioned. I took the name of O'Connor from the transfer. All this occurred on Saturday, the 11th August. On the 20th of August, I went to the Bank for the purpose of stopping payment of the £100 note. The name "Charles James Baker" was on the note at the time when I handed it over to Mr. Bassett.

The witness was cross-examined by Mr. Sergeant Wilkins, but nothing material was elicited.

George Lintorn examined by the Attorney-General: I am a share-dealer. I have had dealings with Killick and Company. I was at their office about half-past eleven o'clock on the morning of Saturday, the 11th August, when a person came to sell twenty Eastern Counties shares. I went into the private room where the stranger and Mr. Bassett were. I did not take particular notice of the stranger, but I remember this transfer being executed by him. I saw the stranger write it. I cannot say that I should know him again. There was nobody in the private room but the stranger, Bassett, and myself. I saw the £100 note handed over to the same person who signed the transfer.

Some questions were put in cross-examination to the witness by Mr. Sergeant Wilkins, but they failed to shake the testimony given in the examination in chief.

MR. GRIFFIN'S EVIDENCE.

Mr. Griffin, examined by Mr. Bodkin: I am a clerk in the Bank of England. This £100 note was brought on Saturday, the 11th August, to the Bank to be exchanged. The name and address now on the back of it were on it when it was received there. I gave the bearer of the note 50 sovereigns, and a ticket which would entitle him to get notes in another department of the Bank. This is the ticket which I gave to the party. It is the practice of the Bank to require the name and address of the party changing a note. The name and address given were Frederick Manning, 7, New Weston-street, Bermondsey.

Another witness from the Bank of England proved that he gave in exchange for the ticket referred to by the last witness five £10 notes, numbered 67,372 to 67,376 inclusive.

John Blatchford, examined by the Attorney-General: I was for several years attorney to the late Patrick O'Connor. The signature to the transfer (of the Eastern Counties shares) is not in his handwriting.

Henry Barnes recalled: I walked from Minver-place to Greenwood-street, Mile-end-road, and I also went there in an omnibus and in a cab. It took me forty-two minutes to walk there, thirty-five minutes to go in an omnibus, and twenty-five minutes in a cab.

Cross-examined by Mr. Ballantine: I have not measured the distance.

James King, examined by the Attorney-General: On Friday, the 10th August, the postman brought me, at the London Docks, the letter now shown to me. I gave it to Lackington to take it to O'Connor's house.

Lackington, a messenger of the London Docks, proved that he left the letter at 21, Greenwood-street.

Richard Welsh, who was examined yesterday, and who then stated that he delivered the lime bought by Manning to the female prisoner, was now recalled, at the instance of Ballantine, and admitted that he might be mistaken in that respect, but he believed that it was the female prisoner to whom he gave the lime.

This closed the evidence for the prosecution.

THE DEFENCE.

Mr. Sergeant Wilkins then rose, and, addressing the Jury, said: I appear before you to-day as the counsel for the male prisoner, Manning. I am here as his advocate, and therefore, no doubt, you will watch with jealousy—and justly so—any observations which I may urge upon his behalf. I do not complain of that. Every man who stands forward as the advocate in any such case ought to be watched carefully. But, at the same time, I need not remind you that it is your duty, also, to weigh well any observations I may present to you, and to give them that attention which they deserve. I ask no more. When I announce to you that I appear before you as the advocate of the male prisoner, Manning, you will at once perceive that I stand in a position unequalled in the history of criminal trials. My difficulties are immense. The mere accusation itself against any man argues a foregone conclusion in nine cases out of ten, and renders his defence a task which is always extremely arduous. What, then, is my position? In the first place, I have to answer the first counsel of the land. In the next place, I have to urge upon you a line of defence which, at first sight, appears very odious; and, in the next place, I am to be followed—strange as it may appear—by another defending counsel, whose duty it will be to neutralise, as far as in him lies, all that I may urge, and to destroy, if he can, the man whom I wish to save. Whatever topics he may urge upon you, however, I shall not quarrel with them. However strenuously he may labour on behalf of his client, and however painful I may feel my situation, I must award to him that meed of approbation which is due to a faithful discharge of duty. But my difficulties do not end here. How does it happen that, while, as a people, we are boasting of the liberties we possess, and the securities which those liberties afford us—how does it happen, I ask, that a case of this kind is never tried, but even the counsel for the Crown and the learned Judge on the bench himself, feel called upon to caution you against impressions previously made—to caution you

D

against the efforts of those who set themselves up as the defenders of our liberties, but who, in such cases, do all they can to prejudice your minds, to pervert your path, to dam up the streams of justice, and prejudge the case by urging upon the public topics and circumstances which ought never to weigh with you for a moment, but which, nevertheless, have an effect upon your minds, whether you will or no? You were told by the Attorney-General, who I am happy to say, in passing, has conducted this case in a manner which reflects the greatest credit upon him—he told you (quoting the language of a celebrated Judge) to forget all you had heard and read on this subject, and to come with your minds unprejudiced and unbiassed to the decision of a case which I may say involves at once the temporal and eternal interests of two of our fellow-creatures. Who are they that render these precautions necessary? Who are the rebels against justice? Who are they that transgress the law? Who are the men who dare to dictate to a Court and Jury, and who seek to intimidate you into a particular verdict, because it squares with prejudices resulting from an imperfect knowledge of the whole history of the case? I have read with deep interest that frightful event, the French revolution—an event that did more at once to ennoble and to debase, to dignify and to degrade the human race, than any other event with which I am acquainted; and I have found that what adds to the horrors of each stage of cruelty, as it presents itself to our view, is, that a depraved press prejudged every case before its investigation, making the trial a meaningless form and an empty pageant. I call upon you, as far as in you lies, to treat with contempt the *dicta* to which I have referred; to push them entirely from your sight, couched though they be in good language, and aided by all the influence of a wide circulation —to treat them with ignominy and English indignation, and come to the inquiry with a calm, unimpassioned, and a peaceful mind. But I fear that in asking this, I am asking you to un- man yourselves—for it is impossible for you to break asunder entirely the band of prejudice which has been entwined around your minds from week to week. I implore you, I entreat you, however, to give the case your most careful and unbiassed attention. I don't dictate to you what your verdict shall be. It would be arrogant in me to do so—it is no part of my duty. My duty is to watch my adversary, to see that he take no unfair advantage of my client; to see that whatever is attempted to be proved against him, if proved at all, is proved in a proper manner; and to urge upon you every topic which I may think entitled to your attention; and, having done so, my duty ceases. You have then your duty to discharge, and it is no easy one. The problem before you is not one which can be solved in a moment. It is not a problem that can be solved by impulse or strong feeling; neither can it be solved by impressions made upon your minds before coming into court. Considering, then, the importance of the case, and the sacred obligation under which you have become bound, to give a just verdict in it, I trust that it will not be regarded as affectation in me, or be thought that I am asking too much, when I implore you to s ek light from more than human wisdom in the solution of the question, and to exercise all the care, and caution, and self-possession, and judgment which you can bring to bear upon it. I do not seek to set your feelings against your judgment; I only desire to awaken your senses, that you may give a better judgment. I ask you to look at the consequences of your verdict:—to consider the result of the investigation—because it reaches from earth to futurity—to a futurity never ending. I ask you to let nothing dissuade you from doing your duty; I do not seek to steal a verdict from your cowardice; I ask merely that you should act dispassionately and calmly—that you should look and pause at every fact, and give it your most solemn attention. Having said thus much, let me now ask you to look at the case itself. What is the nature of the defence? It is the defence which he (Manning) himself set up the moment he was apprehended—the defence in which he has persevered up to the present time. That defence I shall seek to substantiate by reason, argument, and evidence, and leave you to form your own conclusions on it. I shall not attempt to quarrel with the law as laid down by the Attorney-General. I shall not dispute that his view of it was a very correct one. The first question we have to consider is, was O'Connor murdered at all? I fear there is but little doubt on that point. I fear that no one who has heard the evidence can have the slightest doubt that the wretched man O'Connor— who excites our sympathies only because he was hurried in so awful a manner from time into eternity—I say there can be little doubt that he was murdered by some one. The questions then arise—When? where? how? and by whom? The theory on the part of the prosecution is, that he was murdered on the afternoon of Thursday, the 9th of August, although that is by no means proved. I admit, however, that probability points to that time. Then, where was he murdered? That is by no means so clear. It is said on the other side that he was murdered in the house of the two prisoners; and then comes the next question—How was he murdered? That I think is proved beyond a doubt by the medical evidence. Then comes the important question—Was he murdered by both? If so, where is the evidence of their concert? As far as the male prisoner is concerned, there is not a single fact from beginning to end to justify the hypothesis on the other side, that he premeditated the destruction of O'Connor. It seems to me—and I have read the case with great interest and attention—that the only circumstances that can be urged against the male prisoner, Manning, as arguing anything like premeditation, are the purchases of the lime and the crow-bar. Now, let me invite your attention to these two facts. My hypothesis is one which at first sight may appear shocking and unseemly; but we must not allow the usual ur- banities of life to interfere with our judgment on questions like the present. We are all

D

in the habit of associating the female character with the idea of mildness and obedience, and that of the male with the idea of power and strength. It is not necessary, however, to come to the conclusion that this rule is an universal one. History teaches us that the female is capable of reaching higher in point of virtue than the male, but that when once she gives way to vice, she sinks far lower than our sex. My hypothesis, then, is, that the female prisoner Manning premeditated, planned, and concocted the murder, and that she made her husband her dupe and instrument for that purpose. The learned sergeant then proceeded to call the attention of the Jury to the facts of the case in support of this hypothesis. With respect to the purchase of the lime, he held that Mrs. Manning had suggested to her husband that lime was necessary to destroy the slugs in the garden, and had got him to purchase it for that purpose; that, in doing so, he made no secret of the purchase, as he might easily have done had he entertained any criminal intention. If he had wanted the lime secretly he might easily have carried it home himself, or gone to a remote district for it; instead of which he obtained it in the neighbourhood, told the purpose for which he wanted it, and wrote with his own hand the address to which it was to be sent. It was worthy of notice, too, he thought, that although it was not taken home for two days, he manifested no impatience for it. Was there any evidence of mystery in all that? Then, with respect to the crow-bar. Where did the male prisoner go for that? There were plenty of receivers of stolen goods, calling themselves "dealers in marine stores," and living in dark passages, where such an instrument as that for an unhallowed purpose might have been obtained. But, instead of going there, he went to one of the most respectable ironmongers in London, Mr. Evans, in King William-street, and ordered it openly, before all the people in the shop, described the sort of instrument he wanted, wrote his name and address, and waited two or three days till one was made. When it was on its way home to him, he met the boy with it on the bridge. The press, by way of amusing the public, had described Manning as a conceited, consequential sort of man. It might be so. These things were the result of accident and constitutional conformation. What was more likely than that this same feeling of conceit had prompted Manning to say to the boy that surely paper was a scarce thing in his shop, and then to go to a stationer's shop and buy one paper to wrap it in? He begged the Jury to observe that Mrs. Manning knew the crow-bar was coming, that she received it at the house, and showed that she knew where it was bought, what was to be paid for it, and that she paid another shilling, because it happened to be larger than was expected. What was that bought for? It was absurd to suppose that it was purchased for the purpose of the murder, because, with a poker and a pistol in the house, it was not necessary to have it to deprive him of life. It was equally unnecessary to lift the stones of the kitchen, for a meat-chopper or a pair of tongs sharpened with wear would have done that equally well. If such an instrument had been wanted for the purpose of the murder, it was impossible not to suppose that its purchase would have been effected with much greater secrecy. These were the only two circumstances which occurred before the event which seemed to afford anything like a case on the part of the prosecution against Manning. Was the murder, then, done by the two prisoners? The circumstances, both before and after the events seemed to lead an opposite conclusion. There was nothing to show concert before; there was everything to show the opposite of concert after. Both went off in different directions; they were never seen to speak to each other, or to be in each other's company afterwards. Was the murder, then, done by one person? There was no doubt in the world that it could have been; for, supposing O'Connor shot with the pistol, any one with the strength of childhood could have completed the act. The burying could, with equal ease, have been effected by one person. If it was done by one person, then what was the motive for it? What motive could Manning have? The counsel for the prosecution had tried to make it appear that Manning was jealous of O'Connor. In his (Mr. Sergeant Wilkins's) opinion, Manning was not the man to be jealous. No man who had read the history of the case could doubt that Manning was only too easy about his honour as a husband. It was evident that he allowed his wife night after night to visit O'Connor alone—that he received him upon every occasion with the greatest cordiality and friendship. No one had proved that even an angry word had taken place between them, or that he was unwilling to receive his visits. On the very last occasion they were seen in company with each other, they appeared to be on the most friendly terms. Where was Manning's motive for murdering him, then? Could it be said that Manning was influenced by the love of lucre—that he did it in order to possess himself of O'Connor's property? Let facts speak for themselves. It did not appear that Manning possessed himself of a shilling that belonged to O'Connor, or the slightest tittle of his property. With respect to the £100 note, he would show, by-and-by, that he was in that case the mere dupe of his wife, as he had been throughout the whole affair. He was aware that with regard to Manning's defence there might be a great deal of declamation. It might be said, as it had been said, that he was crowning himself with infamy by throwing the blame upon the wife. That was justly said; but if the blame was justly due to his wife—if it was she alone who committed the murder, had not the husband suffered enough from her already, without having another allowing himself to be sacrificed by the wicked woman who had entrapped him? [He] would show from the evidence, as he proceeded, that she was not only soundly capable of this murder, this act, but of facing it out in a manner that he was happy to say few people could. And then he called the Jury's attention to the fact that it was Mrs. Manning who wrote the notes inviting O'Connor to dinner, who was constantly with him at his lodgings, and who had access to his secrets. According to the testimony of Mr. Keating, O'Connor, was seen, about a quarter to five o'clock, on Thursday, on London-bridge, going in the direction of Minver-place. The Jury would be able to form their own opinion, from the evidence, as to the time it would be likely to occupy the deceased in walking from the Surrey side of the bridge to Manning's house. On Friday, the 12th of August, Keating called at Manning's house. At that time O'Connor was dead. Whom did Keating see? Let the Jury mark that. He saw Mrs. Manning. Let the Jury observe her hypocrisy—her falsehood—her consummate wickedness. Keating asked Mrs. Manning if she had seen O'Connor. She replied that she had not seen him since Wednesday night. Keating said it was a very strange thing. "Very strange," repeated the female prisoner, "for I invited him to dinner on the Thursday, and Mr. Manning thought it a most ungentlemanly thing that he did not come at the appointed time. I went to his lodgings to ascertain the reason why he did not come." On that occasion—the only time when her lip was noticed to quiver and her cheek to blanch—she made use of an expression which had struck him, as he saw it had done some of the Jury. She said, "Poor Mr. O'Connor! he was the best friend I had in the world." "Poor Mr. O'Connor!" (continued the learned sergeant). Why "Poor Mr. O'Connor?" You (apparently addressing the female prisoner) knew his body was mouldering in your kitchen. You knew you were at that moment in possession of his property. You knew his voice would never be heard again. You knew that he had been hurried out of time into eternity. Well might you say, "Poor Mr. O'Connor," thrown off your guard at the moment. If you believed merely that he had gone out of town in some freak of fancy—for you describe him as a fitful and fanciful person—why exclaim "Poor Mr. O'Connor?" Was it true that the woman who exclaimed "Poor Mr. O'Connor"—who affected to be astonished that he had not kept an appointment to dine with her on Thursday—had at that moment possession of O'Connor's property? Had she his shares, money, and scrip in her possession? How did she become possessed of them? His box was locked; he always carried his keys in his pocket; how did she get those keys? How did she get those keys but from O'Connor's pocket; and, if from his pocket, how did she get access to his pocket? The Attorney-General seemed to think that the female prisoner did not possess herself of O'Connor's property on the Thursday. Why, then, should she have been at O'Connor's lodgings for an hour on that day? Why did she come down pale and trembling? It might be that there was more property than she could take away that day. It might be that she thought it more prudent to take a portion on Thursday and a portion on Friday. One thing, however, is clear—she knew where O'Connor kept his property; and it is equally clear that she was afterwards found in possession of it. The evidence of David Graham agreed almost to the letter with that of Mr. Keating, and he (Mr. Sergeant Wilkins) therefore thought it unnecessary to refer to it. James Coleman had stated that he saw O'Connor on the 9th of August, about ten minutes after five o'clock, within 150 yards of Minver-place, and going towards Manning's house. He (Mr. Sergeant Wilkins) thought, therefore, that the witness Younghusband must have been mistaken when he said he saw O'Connor at a quarter past five on London-bridge going towards the City. If O'Connor had gone to the house of the prisoners to dinner, as no doubt he had done, why had he turned away? If Mrs. Manning, as she represented, had gone to O'Connor's lodgings to fetch him, she must have left her own house before five o'clock; for it was clear that, within a few minutes of that hour, O'Connor was almost at the prisoner's door. There was no evidence who let O'Connor into the house in Minver-place on that day; but it was clear that, if Mrs. Manning was at home, he would not be turned from the door; and it was evident, from her own statement, that she was at home at six o'clock; for she said that at that hour she left her house to go to O'Connor's lodgings in Greenwood-street. The next witness was Sophia Payne, who had proved that on Thursday, the 9th of August, at a quarter before seven o'clock in the evening, she saw Manning sitting on the garden-wall of his house. Now, he (Mr. Sergeant Wilkins) would not say that the male prisoner might not, after the commission of the murder, have aided and assisted in secreting the body. He would not say that, after the deed was done, Manning might not—partly from fear, and partly, perhaps, from some regard for the woman—have assisted her in disposing of the body; but he contended there was nothing to show that Manning was aware of the contemplated murder, or that he participated in the act. It might be that, as early as seven o'clock, or thereabouts, Manning was at the place, and that he had taken steps to conceal a deed which, if brought to light, would have hazarded his own life, let him be innocent as the most innocent. How did Manning appear at that time, according to the statements of the witnesses? He wore his ordinary dress, and presented, in all respects, his usual aspect. No blood or stains were seen upon his clothing—nothing to indicate that he had been engaged in the commission of the deed. It appeared that Manning sat on the wall for twenty minutes or half-an-hour, smoking and drinking, and then got down, saying that he must go to dress, as he had an engagement. He (Mr. Sergeant Wilkins) thought he would be able to show that Mrs. Manning had, from the beginning to the end, taken as much pains to impose upon and cheat her husband as to cheat any one else. There seemed to be little doubt that the murder was committed on the Thursday, and on the Monday afterwards the male prisoner was at Bainbridge's, the broker's, and about five o'clock in the afternoon requested Bainbridge's servant to fetch his wife to tea. Could the Jury have any doubt that Manning at that time really believed that his wife was at home? The servant came back, and said she could not find the place. Manning then went himself—and how did he act? When he got to the house he knocked at the door, but got no answer. He then, not knowing that any one was looking at him, knocked at the window. Could they have any doubt that he expected his wife would answer him? She did not answer. Manning then asked a woman whom he saw standing at a door opposite, whether she had seen his wife? The woman replied that she had gone away in a cab, taking with her a great deal of luggage. It was clear there could have been no concert between Mrs. Manning and her husband as to where she should go, for she told Mr. Moxhay, when he apprehended her in Edinburgh, and asked her where her husband was, that she did not know, for she left him in London on a sudden, without his knowledge. It would probably be attempted to be shown, on the part of Mrs. Manning, that she was upon terms of peculiar intimacy with O'Connor—that he was what was commonly called "a very good friend" to her. Experience had shown them that the man who forgot the obligations of life, as the unhappy deceased appeared to have done, might count upon the hollowness and deceitfulness of the wicked woman with whom he was associated. He (Mr. Sergeant Wilkins) had no doubt that the female prisoner and O'Connor were upon terms of endearment—that she might have put eau de Cologne upon his head—that she might have said he was to her as a father. When they were together, there were, no doubt, all those outward manifestations of regard; but could any one suppose that Mrs. Manning entertained any real affection for O'Connor? This question naturally occurred to every mind:—"What! you love O'Connor? Why, then, did you rob his pockets? Why did you steal his property? Why did you conceal his death?" If Manning still entertained any regard or affection for his wife, he (Mr. Sergeant Wilkins) could understand why he might have concealed O'Connor's death. But if O'Connor were Mrs. Manning's friend—if she loved him better than her husband—though it might have been an unholy love—she would not have been the person to conceal his death. If she had really loved O'Connor, and had seen him struck down by the hand of him whom she despised, she would without hesitation have given up the murderer to justice, and would not have crept slily to the dead man's room, have possessed herself of his property, and have gone to Edinburgh, to endeavour to convert it into money. It might be supposed that there had been jealousy of O'Connor on the part of Manning. He (Mr. Sergeant Wilkins) was not there to defend that which no man of proper principle could countenance; and he was afraid that Manning might have deserved contempt for having lent himself to his own dishonour, and sanctioned intimacies and approaches which every good man would scout. The next witnesses were Anne and Emily Armes—two young women whose characters, he believed, were without a stain, but against whom his learned friend (Mr. Ballantine) had been instructed to insinuate that they were reaping the wages of shame, and letting out their house for improper purposes. On the Friday evening previous to the murder, Mrs. Manning was with O'Connor at his lodgings, where a quantity of scrip was laid upon the table, and he described to her its character and objects. It appeared that she was at that time wheedling and coaxing O'Connor to give her an account of the scrip, and the best mode of disposing of it. After reading passages from the evidence of the two witnesses Anne and Emily Armes, Mr. Sergeant Wilkins, alluding to the visit paid by Mrs. Manning to O'Connor's lodgings on Thursday, the 9th of August, asked why she had stayed there for an hour, when, according to her own story, she had reason to suppose that O'Connor was at her house? The next witness was William Massey, and he asked the particular attention of the Jury to the evidence of this man. The Attorney-General, and the community, seemed to have been led to suppose that Massey was to prove something very wonderful, while he (Mr. Sergeant Wilkins) thought the Jury would be of opinion that his evidence really amounted to nothing. Massey was a medical student, and the statements which had been mentioned by the Attorney-General as the result of one conversation, turned out to have been scraps and fragments of different conversations held at various times; and those observations naturally and necessarily arose out of topics which happened to be the subjects of conversation. For instance, it appeared that the male prisoner asked Massey whether he thought murderers went to heaven. That certainly seemed an odd question to ask; but it appeared that a conversation had previously taken place about the exhibition of a wax figure of Rush at Madame Tussaud's, which had suggested this singular enquiry. He (Mr. Sergeant Wilkins) could not help thinking, though he had no wish to injure Madame Tussaud, that her exhibition, in immortalising such villains as Rush, was a great nuisance. Massey stated that, being a medical student, conversations connected with his profession had frequently taken place between Manning and himself, and that Manning on one occasion asked him where he thought the seat of the human brain was. One certainly could not help thinking it a very absurd thing for any man who knew anything of the animal formation to ask such a question. [At this observation the features of the female prisoner—who had previously maintained a serious and rather melancholy expression of countenance—relaxed into a smile, which she, however, quickly repressed.] According to Massey's statement, he and Manning were one day talking about fire-arms, when the latter asked Massey if he had ever fired an air-gun? and at another time Manning said he would like to get O'Connor, who was very rich, to put his name to a promissory note for £500, and that he thought the best way to get him into a good-humoured mood would be to induce him to take brandy and water. When a man was accused of crimes of this nature, it would really be amusing—but for the seriousness of the investigation—to mind the ingenuity which was displayed in raising up every trifling act as evidence of his guilt. Why, every one of these observations was just as likely to be made by any man in Manning's situation as by Manning himself, and that with the most innocent intentions. The witness William Cahill proved that a shovel was bought by Mrs. Manning on the 8th of August, the very day on which she had invited O'Connor to dine. They then had the evidence of the poor child Hannah Firman, whose testimony had not been impugned; and he thought the only effect of the cross-examination to which she had been subjected ought to be to excite the sympathies of those who heard it to endeavour to snatch her from sin and ruin. The learned Sergeant then proceeded to refer to the evidence of Mr. and Mrs. Bainbridge, observing that it was quite clear they had mistaken the observation Manning made when he returned from looking for his wife. Mr. Bainbridge positively asserted that Manning said, "I have started my mistress off into the country." Now, was it not more probable that Manning said his wife had started into the country? Then Mrs. Bainbridge said she would swear Manning's observation was, "I have sent my mistress into the country;" while Matilda Weldon, the servant, would not swear whether Manning said he had sent his wife, or that she had gone. It was clear Mr. and Mrs. Bainbridge were mistaken, because Manning had not started his wife into the country; he did not know that she had gone, or that she was going. Was it likely, if Manning had been a participator in the crime, that he would have quietly allowed his wife to go off, he knew not where, taking with her all she could carry? and that he would then have said he had sent her into the country? The story Mrs. Manning told herself showed that the Bainbridges were mistaken; for she said, on her apprehension, that she left London without her husband's knowledge, and that she did not know at the time whether she was going to Edinburgh or France. It appeared to him (Mr. Sergeant Wilkins) that the explanation of Manning's present difficulty was afforded by his own observation to one of the police officers—"I was a great fool that I did not stop and explain all." Now, it was no uncommon thing for innocent people, when danger stared them in the face, and when they found themselves involved in a mesh from which it seemed impossible for them to extricate themselves, to have recourse to conduct which might be considered as proof of their guilt. Cases had occurred in this metropolis, where persons of high respectability had been stopped by scoundrels, who had threatened to accuse them of certain crimes unless money or valuables were given to them. If the person assailed were a man of great energy and of high moral courage he would at once seize his ruffianly assailant by the throat, and deliver him up to justice; but, if he were a nervous and excitable man, rather than labour under the imputation of such a charge, he would take his watch from his pocket, and give it to the scoundrel. Now the all-charitable, deep-reflecting world would say that the fact of a man's giving up his watch under such circumstances was a proof of his guilt; but men who had had experience in investigations of this description would form a very different conclusion, for they knew that to the superficial, innocent men often appeared guilty, while the hardened and wicked, and guilty were regarded as innocent. Now, he would put the present case to the Jury in this aspect:—Manning might have been sitting up-stairs in the dining-room, while his wife went down-stairs and shot O'Connor through the head; Manning would be horror-stricken; he would say, "At the very bottom of the stairs of this room the woman has destroyed a fellow-creature; what am I to do? If I go out and proclaim her guilt, I shall be her destruction. The world may accuse me of committing the deed, or it may be said that as I was in the house when it was done it may be fairly presumed that I had the opportunity of preventing it." The unfortunate man might yield to bad reasoning, by which hundreds had been enmeshed, and might determine not to give the criminal up to justice. He (Mr. Sergeant Wilkins) did not know what the truth was, but it might be that Manning had assisted in disposing of the body; but that would not make him guilty of the crime with which he was now charged. It might be that Manning's fears had led him to adopt a line of conduct which had involved him in difficulties; but the explanation seemed to be afforded in the few words he had uttered to the officers, "I am perfectly innocent; I am a great fool that I came away without explaining it." It appeared from Manning's conduct that he had been inclined to linger about the spot, with the view, probably, of telling what he knew, for he did not quit London till the Wednesday, although inquiries were made after him on the Sunday, and a still more eager search on the Monday and Tuesday. It appeared that he had entertained some intention of returning, for he had left with a friend a new hat, which he might easily have taken with him. Mr. Sergeant Wilkins then briefly alluded to the evidence of Mary Scholefield, William Kirk, William Day, and Mr. Moxhay, the superintendent of police at Edinburgh, observing, that he might congratulate that city upon possessing so excellent an officer. Never since he had been in the profession had he (Mr. Sergeant Wilkins) heard a man in his capacity give his evidence in so intelligent a manner, and so creditably to himself. Mr. Moxhay told them that Mrs. Manning had been a consistent character throughout. That woman certainly must have the most extraordinary control over herself of any person of whom he (Mr. Sergeant Wilkins) had ever heard. She treated Mr. Moxhay with all the courtesy of the drawing-room. When he observed that his impression was that she was Mrs. Manning, she still retained the utmost self-possession. Mr. Moxhay asked if she had any objection to her luggage being searched? She said, "Certainly not." She was asked if she had any receipt

"Scrip? what is scrip? said she, as if it were the first time she had ever heard it mentioned; while it was proved that she had received from O'Connor a full and accurate description of it. Mr. Moxhay opened one of her boxes, and the first thing he found was a bill with the name of "F. G. Manning" upon it. Still she retained her self-possession. "Now have you any scrip?" she was asked. "Oh yes," said she, "to be sure—scrip of my own." She was told that she was apprehended on the charge of murdering Mr. O'Connor. "Murder Mr. O'Connor!" she exclaimed; "No, indeed; he was the best friend I had in the world. He was like a father to me." If Mr. O'Connor had been like a father to her, she certainly had behaved very unlike a child towards him. Mr. Moxhay asked where her husband was? She replied, "Upon my honour, I don't know. He ill-treated me, and once attempted to kill me. I came away from London suddenly, without his knowing it, and I had not made up my mind where to go to." Then, if her husband had treated her so ill, and if she was so fond of Mr. O'Connor, why did she not, from love of him, or from hatred of her husband, denounce Manning as O'Connor's murderer? The learned sergeant then read the evidence of police-sergeant Langley, who apprehended the male prisoner, and who stated that Manning remarked, "I suppose they will find a great deal of money upon my wife—£1300 or £1400 at least." The sum found upon her, it appeared, was only about £150, so that it was clear Manning knew nothing of the amount of the money. The male prisoner said, on his apprehension, that "his wife shot O'Connor; she invited him to dinner; and when he came she suggested to him that he should go down to wash his hands; and, when at the bottom of the stairs, she put one hand on his shoulder and shot him at the back of the head with the other." Now, who could say that all this was not possible? Much as Manning might detest the crime, yet his feelings as a husband and as a man might prompt him to seek to screen his wife. Captain Chevalier asked him, in Jersey, what had become of the body, and he said, "She had a grave dug for him." Manning asked, if his wife were to confess, would he be free? and to that question the officer gave a very proper answer. Manning then observed, "I am sure she would confess in the presence of a clergyman." A shooting-coat of Manning's had been produced, in which there was found some tissue paper and loose gunpowder; but it was not known how long it might have been since he had worn that coat; and if, when he kept an hotel at Taunton, he had been a sportsman, it was not at all surprising that he should have a few grains of gunpowder in his pocket. If he had really been a murderer, one of the first things he was likely to do would have been to empty his pockets, and get rid of every evidence of his guilt. The learned sergeant proceeded to refer to the evidence of Inspector Haynes, and of Mr. Stephens, the stockbroker, directing the attention of the Jury to the inquiries made by the female prisoner of the latter witness, whether she could sell Sambre and Meuse scrip without the knowledge of her husband. He (Mr. Sergeant Wilkins) thought, then, that he was justified in saying that she was seeking to cheat her husband, as well as everybody else. Could there be any doubt that, at the very time she made these inquiries, she was contemplating stealing the Sambre and Meuse and Amiens and Boulogne shares belonging to O'Connor, and that she had formed the intention of quitting England and abandoning her husband? Mr. Sergeant Wilkins then called attention to the evidence of Mr. Green, clerk of the transfers to the Eastern Counties Railway Company, and said he thought he was justified in expressing an opinion that Mrs. Manning had, throughout the whole transactions, sought to avoid the vigilance of her husband, and to use him as her instrument. He would ask the Jury, on looking at the male prisoner, whether they thought any person who had ever seen him was likely to forget him? Well, it had been proved that some person had gone to the office of Messrs. Killick and Co., and had disposed of some scrip which had belonged to O'Connor, for which he had signed the transfer paper. Mr. Shillibeer had stated that he knew Manning's handwriting well, but that the signature to that paper was not his, and did not resemble it in the slightest degree. Mr. Shillibeer also said that he thought the signature was in the handwriting of the person who had filled up the body of the paper, but that an endeavour had been made to render the writing different in appearance. The witness, however, would not swear that it was Manning who signed the transfer, but he said that he gave in payment to the person who did sign it a £100 Bank of England note, a note for £5, and five sovereigns. The £100 note was afterwards presented at the Bank of England, but there was no evidence that Manning was the person by whom it was presented, although his name was upon it. Could there be any doubt that his wife had induced him to write his name on it? It was clear that if Manning was the person who had forged O'Connor's name to the transfer, he would not have gone to the Bank of England, or have written his name upon the note, and so have placed upon the proceeds of his forgery the clue to his detection. But, with all the fearlessness of a man who had nothing to dread, he had written his name and address on the back of the note. Where were the proceeds of that note afterwards found? In the possession of Mrs. Manning, when she was apprehended at Edinburgh. He (Mr. Sergeant Wilkins) had now gone through all the evidence, and if he had omitted to notice anything, he must ask the Jury to supply his deficiencies. He had been called upon to discharge a duty from which, had he consulted his own feelings, he would have shrunk. Not that he was oppressed with a consciousness of the guilt of his client, or bowed down by the real difficulties of his case, but that he had to fight against a mass of prejudice which had been created by those who ought to have known better; that he knew the interest which attached to the case from the manner in which it had been written up; and that he felt it most lacerating and agonizing to stand there as the representative of the husband, criminating and seeking to convict the wife. This was to him such a task that it had almost unfitted him for the important duties which devolved upon him. The Jury had, however, listened to him with the greatest attention, and he was sure they would weigh what he had said with care, diligence, and caution. He prayed them, by all they held sacred, as they valued the trust which their country had reposed in them, as they respected its laws, as they wished to maintain the proper administration of justice, as they loved our common manhood, and as they expected to be judged, that, whatever their verdict might be—and what it should be he presumed not to dictate to them—it might be a verdict of reason. He called upon them not to allow those common impulses—good, divine, as they were—which influenced them in private life, and induced them to yield affection, protection, and respect to woman, to step in between them and truth, but to treat the matter as a pure abstract question of reasoning, as between two human beings. He would only add, that his client placed himself upon his country with confidence, knowing that his conduct would be weighed by upright men, and that, whatever the verdict might be, it would be in consonance with that honesty and truth which formed the bulwark and protection of English liberties.

A short adjournment took place at the termination of Mr. Sergeant Wilkins's address; when the Judges, the Lord Mayor, and several of the more distinguished persons on the bench, retired to luncheon. During their absence the prisoners were removed from the dock. After an interval of about 20 minutes the learned Judges returned, and, the prisoners having been again placed at the bar,

MR. BALLANTINE'S DEFENCE OF MRS. MANNING.

Mr. Ballantine proceeded to address the Jury on behalf of the female prisoner. He commenced by complimenting the Attorney-General on the fair and temperate manner in which he had opened the case for the prosecution. He could not ask the Jury to dismiss from their minds all that they had heard with reference to this case, for he knew they could not avoid remembering such things; and, when the evidence adduced on the part of the prosecution was concluded, they must have wondered how it was that many allegations relating to this unhappy woman which had found their way into the public prints, and had been openly talked of, had not been proved. It was clear that those allegations could have little foundation in reality, because, as this case had been conducted by able and intelligent officers, who had discharged their duty with great propriety, intelligence, and zeal, they might be certain that the evidence which had been brought forward was all that had any bearing on the subject. He need not refer to the exaggerated reports and calumnies which had been circulated with regard to his client; for he was not surprised at them, after the mode in which the case had been conducted on the part of the other prisoner, and after the attempts which had been made, even before his client came into a court of justice, on the part of one who ought to have cherished and protected her, to place her in such a position as to render it impossible that she could be rescued from the tomb prophesied for her by many. The Jury would not, therefore, be surprised at his (Mr. Ballantine's) attempt to obtain a separate trial for the woman at the bar. He would have been glad to avoid certain observations which he felt bound to make—but which he would endeavour to make, temperately—upon the course pursued by his learned friend, Sergeant Wilkins. He (Mr. Ballantine) would have been glad if they could have escaped the spectacle, unparalleled in a criminal court, of finding an advocate, either for the prosecution or for the defence, in the presence of a person who was undergoing a trial for her life, denouncing her in terms that, to say the least, were utterly unnecessary—terms which he could hardly help calling somewhat coarse. He considered that the presence of the person against whom those observations were made, ought, at all events, to have prevented his learned friend from using them, whatever might be the necessities of his case. Far be it from him to say that his learned friend had not exercised the best judgment that he could apply to this matter—that he had not conscientiously followed the instructions he had received; for he would do his learned friend the credit to believe that he had acted, contrary to his own taste and feeling in performing what he believed to be his duty to his client. His learned friend appeared to anticipate that he (Mr. Ballantine) would follow his example, and endeavour to throw upon the male prisoner the burden of this miserable, this unhappy transaction. God forbid that he should pursue that course! He would far rather never enter that court, or any other, than, in the presence of a fellow-creature awaiting his doom—who might be led from that court to the scaffold, and might soon have to appear before his Creator—he would use such terms as had been applied by his learned friend to the female prisoner. He (Mr. Ballantine) would do that which was his duty as an advocate; but, if his duty as an advocate required that he should cast upon the male prisoner the sort of observations and accusations which had been made against the woman, he would feel that his profession was a disgrace, and that the sooner he abandoned it for some less intolerable, the sooner he would be a respected, an honest, an honourable, and an cationable man, and ought him an unsuitable matter to respect himself. Every advocate who was called upon to defend a cause must take the evidence that had been submitted to the Jury. He must shew how that evidence weighed, and, as far as his humble abilities enabled him, point out to the Jury the mode in which he desired them to view it. If that evidence inculpated others, it might be necessary to apply some observations to the subject; but when this painful duty was cast upon an advocate, it ought to be performed in a calm and temperate manner. He (Mr. Ballantine) would now proceed to call the attention of the Jury to the facts of this case, attaching no guilt to any one, and would ask them to consider the issues they were called upon to determine with regard to the female prisoner, and whether they could conclude that she was guilty in either of those points of view which had been presented to them in the fair, temperate, and proper opening of the Attorney-General. The Jury had been told that the female prisoner might be found guilty either as a principal, or as an accessory before the fact. He thought, when they considered the circumstances of the case, that they would hesitate before they found her guilty as an accessory. "Accessorial acts, as between husband and wife, were extremely vague. It was very difficult to understand, in the relationship existing between husband and wife, and in the absence of direct and positive testimony, how far the one might be accessory to what was done by the other. He could not help thinking, then, that, unless they were clearly of opinion that the woman was present at the murder, they would find it almost impossible to come to a satisfactory verdict that she was guilty as an accessory before the fact. He would ask them to consider whether the facts which had been disclosed did not show that, at the time the murder was committed, the female prisoner was not present. He wished first to dispose of that which could alone support the count charging the woman as a principal, present, and aiding and abetting, at the murder; and, if he did that, it would materially assist him in getting them to the conclusion that she might not have been a party acting accessorily in the matter. He hoped the Jury would come to the conclusion that this woman did not forget her sex, and do that which few women were recorded to have done—commit a cold-blooded and atrocious murder, under circumstances of cold-blooded and atrocious violence. What were the circumstances of the case? Mr. O'Connor seemed to have formed a connexion with Mrs. Manning, of the nature of which no one could entertain any doubt. It appeared from the statement of Mrs. Manning herself that her husband had ill-used her, and that ill-usage was not likely to strengthen any feelings of virtue she might possess. He (Mr. Ballantine) would ask the Jury whether it was likely that a woman in the situation of the female prisoner, who had formed a connexion of this nature with O'Connor, would lend herself to the violence imputed to her? It seemed that O'Connor was past the middle age, and it was almost proverbial that at that time of life men were weak enough to yield anything to the women with whom they were connected. Mrs. Manning could have no necessity for committing an act of violence, for there would, no doubt, be moments when she could find her way to O'Connor's coffers without contracting any other guilt than that which attached to the impure and illegal connexion she was maintaining. What motive, then, could there be on the part of Mrs. Manning for engaging in a design for the murder of O'Connor? He thought he had a right to assume either that Mrs. Manning was a woman of abandoned character, ready to resort to any means to attain her ends—and, in that case, she would have had no need to commit murder in order to get possession of O'Connor's property—for she might, undoubtedly, had she chosen, have been taken into comparatively wealthy keeping—or she was a woman of kindly feeling and disposition and in that case her connexion with O'Connor would make it most unlikely that she would lend herself to such a transaction as that with which she was now charged. It appeared that, on the 9th of August, the deceased was seen on London-bridge about five o'clock, in Weston-street at ten minutes after five, and again on London-bridge at a quarter-past five. He appeared then to be vacillating in opinion as to whether he should go to the Mannings or not; but he (Mr. Ballantine) thought the Jury would probably agree with him in believing that this vacillation ended by his turning back and going to Minver-place, where he would not arrive until later than he had been expected. The dinner-hour of the Mannings was generally five o'clock, and, as O'Connor was seen on London-bridge at a quarter-past five, he could not have arrived at Minver-place until considerably after the usual dinner-hour. This would, then, be consistent with the statement of Mrs. Manning, that, finding he did not come at the expected time, she went to look for him at his house in Greenwood-street. According to the statements of the Misses Armes, who were evidently not very favourably disposed towards the female prisoner, she arrived at their house on that evening at a quarter before six, and remained till a quarter-past seven. The distance from Minver-place to Greenwood-street appeared to be about three miles, so that it would probably take Mrs. Manning nearly three-quarters of an hour to go from one place to the other. If she had started from her own house about a quarter-past five o'clock, she might have arrived in Greenwood-street at about a quarter to six. If, then, the murder was committed between half-past five and a quarter to eight o'clock, it was quite impossible that the female prisoner could have been a party to it, for during that time she was absent from her own house. Then, was the murder committed during that period? He thought the evidence that the prosecution would adduce led to no other hypothesis than that it was committed before Manning was seen on there shutting his gate, at a quarter-past seven o'clock. He submitted that all the evidence tended to show that when Mrs. Manning returned home (which, according to the evidence of the Misses Armes, could not be much before a quarter to eight o'clock, the murder had been effected. The next question was, whether Mrs. Manning was an accessory to the murder before the fact. She was charged in the indictment as an accessory before the fact, the supposition on the part of the Crown undoubtedly being, that the probability was, that a murder of this kind was much more likely to have been committed by a man than by a woman. Mr. Sergeant Wilkins had contended that this was a murder which must have been committed by one person, and in that proposition he (Mr. Ballantine) entirely agreed; but it was for the Jury to consider whether it was most probable that such a murder had been committed by a man or a woman. There were three points alleged on the part of the Crown as showing that the woman was an accessory before the fact; namely, that she had been a party to the purchase or order of the crow-bar, the lime, and the shovel. As to the shovel, it was an ordinary coal-shovel, and entirely unfit for the purpose to which it was alleged it was intended to be applied; and, as the prisoners had a garden, why should not Mrs. Manning at once have purchased a spade, which would have been much more serviceable in digging a hole, had she required it for such a purpose? With regard to the lime, Mrs. Manning might have supposed that it was intended for the destruction of the "slugs" which infested the garden; and the woman who paid 1½d. to the boy who took it to the house was not identified by him as the female prisoner. Then as to the crow-bar, which had been ordered by the male prisoner, it had no doubt been paid for by Mrs. Manning, under her husband's directions; and what was a more usual occurrence than for such a payment to be made by the wife in any family in ordinary life? The crow-bar was no doubt brought home wrapped up, fold in fold, in brown paper, and the bill was handed to Mrs. Manning, though how the article was named in the bill did not appear in the evidence. There was nothing whatever in the transaction but might have occurred in the case of any one present; and no man's wife, having been previously informed of the price of an article by her husband, would fail to find fault when she found a higher price charged for the article than had at first been agreed upon. As to the efforts made to throw the whole blame connected with this murder upon the woman, was it to be imagined that this originated with the learned counsel on the other side? It had originated rather in the attempt made by the male prisoner to shift the crime from his own shoulders, if there it rested, to those of the woman he was bound to have protected. It was a mere afterthought, the creation of a feeble mind yielding to the influence of cowardice and fear, and ready, as a poltroon ever was, to preserve his own life at whatever might be the sacrifice. He said this without reference to his guilt or innocence of the crime, and entirely upon the ground of the statements he had himself made, and because of the charge which the learned sergeant had preferred against the wife, and the terms in which that charge was made. He could not understand how any man in the position of a husband, were his wife ever so culpable, even if her guilt was of the deepest dye, could bring himself with so much readiness to cast all blame upon her in the manner which had been exhibited in this instance. He would now come to another point of the case, that which related to the stains of blood said to have been seen on Mrs. Manning's dress. It was very remarkable that the only marks deposed to with respect to one dress were marks upon the cape, and all upon the back of the cape. This he considered inconsistent with the notion that such spots, whatever they were, had been received during the commission of a murder. But so far as the evidence went, these marks were not shown to be blood at all; indeed, he thought they had better evidence than that of the chemist, which led them to believe that the marks were not blood, but iron-mould. There were some other articles besides the cape produced on which the marks of blood were said to be seen. They had toilet covers brought before them of a very handsome description—articles which she had probably obtained possession of in the houses where she had been employed as an upper-servant, houses which indicated that she had been highly respected, and considered as a person altogether unlikely to be mixed up in a transaction of this kind. Now, there were a hundred ways in which toilet covers might get drops of blood upon them. Possibly the person who committed the murder might go to the bed-room after the deed was done, and in this way the marks might be made; or they might be left while taking linen from the drawers, and in a variety of other ways: but all this was nothing to the purpose as implying guilt against the woman at the bar. Then it was said, there was blood on the inside of a dress; but he thought the Jury would have no difficulty in finding an explanation of the fact of there being marks of blood inside the dress of a woman, and that there was nothing in these appearances which could show that the dress was stained at the time of the murder. Therefore, both as regarded the shovel and the stains of blood, he thought the Jury could rest nothing in considering their verdict. Another point to which he would refer was the evidence given by Mr. Massey. That witness seemed to have had some curious conversations with Manning, though they did not affect the case of his client, and these chiefly related to the use of laudanum and chloroform as the mode of getting something out of O'Connor. As to the observations with reference to the will of O'Connor having been made in favour of Mrs. Manning, these seem to have taken place in her presence, and nothing was then said but what she might with the greatest impropriety discredit. With regard to Manning, chloroform, the softest parts of the skull, and the like, these conversations did not take place when the woman was present, as it was probable they would have excited attention and enquiry on her part. He would not say whether they ought to have excited inquiry on the part of Mr. Massey; but this he would observe, that, having had such conversations from time to time with the male prisoner, it would at least have been discreet on his part to mention them, and then probably this awful tragedy would not have occurred, and they would not have been that day sitting to make inquiry into the fate of poor Patrick O'Connor. There was one remarkable circumstance to which he would briefly call the attention of the Jury. The evening of Wednesday the 8th of August was a very important one as regarded this transaction. By that day every one of the articles supposed to have been used in the murder had been purchased. The crow-bar and the lime had been purchased, the conversation with Massey had taken place, and other circumstances had occurred, all going to show that the design of the murder, as laid down in the case for the prosecution, had been completed on the 8th of August. Then what was the conduct of Mrs. Manning on that day? They found that O'Connor had been invited to dinner on that day; and a letter of invitation to him was found in the handwriting of the female prisoner. He would just say, in passing, that, if Manning had intended any evil to O'Connor that night, they could quite understand that he might get another person to write a letter asking him to dinner, and that just in the way she had been made to pay for the crow-bar, Mrs. Manning might have been led to write the letter. On the 8th, however, O'Connor did not come to dinner; but he came in the evening accompanied by a person named Walshe. Now, if at that moment Mrs. Manning had made up her mind to commit a murder, let them recollect what was her demeanour. In the presence of Walshe she asked O'Connor why he had not come, entered into conversation on the subject, and, from beginning to end, exhibited the utmost openness before Walshe, and the most perfect freedom from all concealment. The same evening, when he became faint, what did she do? He would ask if even the worst prostitute could have bathed the temples of a man suffering from giddiness after smoking, with a murderous intent in her heart? At such a moment the heart of even the basest woman would speak out, and she would shrink from going near the man whose murder she had contemplated, and with whom she had lived on terms of the closest intimacy. There was another view to be taken of this matter. Both Manning and his wife were considerably benefited from their acquaintance with O'Connor. Mrs. Manning certainly was greatly benefited, and, in consequence, she would wish to keep up her friendship with him, and to be as much as possible in his company. Throwing aside affection, there was interest in the welfare of O'Connor, and interest of that kind that most affected a woman, and which would lead her to repudiate the notion of murder. He would next ask the Jury to consider the conduct of Mrs. Manning at the house of Miss Armes. Finding that O'Connor did not come to dinner, as she expected, on the 8th, she went to his lodgings to inquire after him, and not to possess herself of his property, as was attempted to be shown. Now, if the hypothesis of the prosecution was correct, the mind of the woman was at that time under influence of the most awful kind that could afflict a human being. With the dreadful weight upon her mind, that she was a party to the murder of a man who had been the friend of her youth, and who, from time to time, had helped her with money, and whose corpse, on her return, she might find buried in her own house—with this awful load pressing upon her mind, she went to the lodgings of O'Connor; and all that the Misses Armes could say of her appearance was, that she looked a little pale. Was such a thing compatible with their ideas of human nature? On the following night, he would admit, it was not improbable that her appearance might indicate that something dreadful had occurred, for it was not impossible that she had then come to the conclusion that some foul deed had been perpetrated; and, accordingly, it was observed that on that occasion she greatly trembled. He would now shortly consider her conduct after the murder had undoubtedly been committed. He would not attempt to deny that at some period or another the woman became acquainted with the murder before she left her house. Whether it was on the Thursday night, or on the Friday, or some days afterwards, it was useless to speculate about; but his impression was, that she learned it previous to her departure for the country. Having learned it, he believed her conduct was consistent and reconcileable with her entire innocence. He had shown why he came to the conclusion that she could not have been present at the murder; he had also shown why he thought it impossible that she could have been accessory before the murder; and he would now endeavour to show that her conduct after it was just such as might have been expected. If she heard of the murder first from her husband, how many views might not be taken of the probable course which she would be inclined to pursue? The criminality which she had clearly indulged in with O'Connor would operate powerfully upon her; she might believe that jealousy was the groundwork on which the conception of the murder had been raised; and the Jury could easily conceive how a woman who had acted sinfully and criminally towards her husband, would shrink from making known a crime which she had good reason to believe had been committed by him on account of the course of life which she herself had pursued. Certain it was that, on the day following the murder, she went to the lodgings of O'Connor, and that there she was seen to exhibit that want of nerve and that shaking of the hand which attracted the notice of the Misses Armes. With reference to the property of O'Connor found in her possession, he was not able to suggest any other reasonable proposition than that, in all probability, he had purchased the scrip but in the Sambre and Meuse Railway; and that she thought herself justified in taking them away; and that, in doing so, she took other property, to which perhaps she thought she was entitled. There was every reason to believe that she wanted to have the money without the knowledge of her husband; and from conversations overheard between her and O'Connor, he had, no doubt, been employed by her to invest that money in railway shares. Placed in such circumstances, and learning that O'Connor was murdered, what was a woman likely to do? Taking the most innocent and virtuous woman in the world, or the most profligate and abandoned, the course which they would adopt on finding that a husband had murdered their friend would depend very much on the temperament of the parties. In the present instance, the woman resolved to get away from her husband, and, while doing so, she possessed herself of a considerable amount of property. He hoped it would be borne in mind that he was not putting this woman before the Jury as a person of pure mind or of pure habits; nor did he regard her as a person guided by high moral feelings. Knowing that O'Connor was murdered, it was not improbable that she immediately resolved upon her course, and went to the house of the deceased to possess herself of her property, and that she took other property, without knowing whether it belonged to her or not. Nothing but scrip was taken away—none of the I.O.U.'s which lay in the cash-box of the deceased. But it was not to be doubted that the husband afterwards got possession of part of the property, and, as he said, sent his wife off to the country. The truth seemed to be, that she resolved to leave him altogether, and that she took the name of Smith in order the better to effect that purpose. There were some smaller matters to which he did not think it necessary to refer; but he trusted that he had shown enough to convince them that the woman at the bar was not accessory before the fact to the murder of this man. In conclusion, the learned counsel thanked the Jury for the attention with which they had listened to his address, and expressed the fullest confidence that the case of his client, though a foreigner, would receive from an English Jury the most patient, careful, and impartial consideration.

The Attorney-General was about to reply, when

Mr. Parry interposed, and said that, although, perhaps, in strictness, the Attorney-General would have the right of reply, yet it was not customary to exercise this power in a case where not a tittle of evidence had been adduced by the prisoners.

The Chief Baron said the Attorney-General clearly had the right.

Mr. Parry then put it to the Attorney-General whether he would exercise the right in a case where the lives of two of his fellow-creatures were at stake?

THE ATTORNEY-GENERAL'S REPLY.

The Attorney-General said he had undoubtedly, as the representative of the Crown, the right to have the last word on an inquiry of this description. It was a right which had been usually exercised with great caution, and he should not in this case have exercised it, though he and many other Attorney-Generals had on other occasions done so, but that he thought it his duty to endeavour to hold as evenly as possible the scales of justice between the parties whose interests were now before the Court. He thought that Mr. Ballantine was justified, in complaining of the course that had been adopted by the learned sergeant. He considered he had only done his duty as an advocate to his client, and he must say that it appeared to him to be the more manly course boldly to state a charge against a party, and the grounds upon which the charge was supported, than to insinuate it, and not have the boldness to openly make the accusation. He concurred entirely in what had been said by both of his learned friends as to the propriety of the Jury dismissing from their minds any impression, but such as was legitimately derived from the evidence laid before them. Both of his learned friends admitted that the unfortunate man O'Connor was murdered by somebody in the house in Minver-place, and that he was murdered either by a shot or by blows, or that death was produced by both jointly. On this point, therefore, there need be no difficulty to the Jury—that in the house occupied by both prisoners, there being no servant to take part in the transaction, Patrick O'Connor was murdered on the 9th of August, either by means of a pistol, or by a crow-bar, or by both. Now, there was, then, one thing on which the learned counsel who had addressed the Court were entirely agreed, and that was that the murder had been committed by one person only. That he thought highly improbable. He did not think that one person could have raised the stones in the kitchen, dug the grave, covered it over, and, above all, could have thrust the body into the grave in the manner which had been described. He did not see any reason why Manning should have committed the murder alone, because, unless he perpetrated it with the concurrence of her whose presence in O'Connor's room would not create suspicion, and thereby obtain the property sought for, he would have no motive for committing the deed. It was not suggested that jealousy was the motive, and they were shut up to the alternative that he was actuated by a desire to get possession of the property of the deceased. How, then, was Manning to get access to the property? Had he gone himself to the lodgings of O'Connor, suspicion might have been excited; but there was one who had been constantly in the habit of going there, whose presence would excite no suspicion whatever. With regard to the time when the murder was alleged to have been committed, there did not appear to be any evidence when it was actually committed; and it was very possible that they might have been committed after the return of the female prisoner from the house of the deceased. A little after five o'clock O'Connor was seen near Minver-place. After that time he was on the bridge, apparently in a hesitating and uncertain mood, very like a person who was looking for some one. The probability, then, was, that, not finding the female prisoner at home, soon after five o'clock, he had left Minver-place, but afterwards returned—whether with the female prisoner or not could not be ascertained; and in all likelihood the murder was committed then. Manning said he was in the house when it was done, but he did not say at what time. He did not say it was committed at five o'clock, or any other hour, having contented himself with saying that he was present, and then attributing the murder to his wife. Was the murder perpetrated, then, before seven o'clock? They had evidence to the effect that the husband was seen smoking his pipe on the garden wall; was it when he was seen to jump from the wall that he went and opened the door to O'Connor, perhaps accompanied by his wife.

Mr. Ballantine: It was half-past seven o'clock when he was seen smoking.

The Attorney-General could only say, from what had come out in evidence, that the murder was not committed at five o'clock, and he had endeavoured to come as near as possible to the time when it was in reality perpetrated. A good deal had been said about the purchase of the chisel, the lime, and the shovel; and it should be borne in mind that before the 8th the chisel and the lime were purchased, and that the shovel was bought on that very day. But then the Mannings were before the 8th in treaty for the sale of their furniture, and they sold it two days after. Why, then, did they buy a shovel on the very day of the murder, when they were actually discussing with a broker whether they should get £13 or £13 10s. for their furniture? No doubt it was used for the removal of the earth from the floor. Mr. Ballantine asked whether the conduct of the woman on the night of the 8th, in the presence of the witness Walshe, was like that of a guilty person. But he did not regard this as a correct view of the matter. On the contrary, she would find that there was no use in attempting concealment, because the fact of a letter having been sent to O'Connor was made known to Walshe. Then, it did not appear that she asked O'Connor, in Walshe's presence, to come to dinner on the Thursday, but she wrote him a letter of invitation after twelve that very night.

Mr. Ballantine: There's no evidence to that effect.

The Attorney-General: He was asked to dinner on the Thursday, but he was not asked in Walshe's presence. Not a word was then said about it; and there was little doubt that an invitation had been sent. It was strange that she should have been so anxious about the matter as to go and fetch him to dinner. But she had not only gone that night, but went also the following, when she, without doubt, opened the boxes of O'Connor by means of the keys that had been taken from his person. It was in evidence that the female prisoner stated that she had herself cleaned the back kitchen on the day of the murder, and therefore she must have been aware of the condition of the kitchen at that time. Then they found her in the custody of Mr. Moxhay at Edinburgh, having in her possession the property of the murdered man. With respect to the man, what was his conduct? He did not deny that he was present at the murder, though he endeavoured to cast the blame upon his wife. He wished it to be implied that he was present when the murder was committed, but that he was present innocently. Was it possible for a man to be present at the commission of murder innocently in such circumstances? Why, only the day after the murder, he went with a part of the property of the murdered man, forged the name of that man, and by this means procured a sum of £110. He then absconded, and, when taken, endeavoured to cast the blame of the whole transaction upon his wife. It was impossible, then, not to come to the conclusion that both prisoners were concerned in this atrocious case. Both were concerned in the purchase of the instruments used in procuring the death and burial of their victim. Both resorted to concealment, and both took part in the distribution of O'Connor's property. He did not complain of his learned friends acting upon their instructions. It was their duty to do all that properly lay within their power for the clients on whose behalf they appeared; but it was equally his duty to endeavour to apply the evidence fairly and impartially, and equally to both parties, without considering what might be the result of the inquiry. He did not intend, when he rose, to trouble them with any minute examination of the different parts of the evidence, nor had he done so; and he would now leave this distressing case in the hands of the Bench and the Jury.

THE JUDGE'S CHARGE.

The Lord Chief Baron then proceeded to deliver his charge to the Jury. The prisoners at the bar, he said, were charged with the awful crime of murder. They had respectively pleaded "Not guilty;" and, when the Jury had considered all the evidence, and heard what the law was upon the subject, they would have to determine with respect to each of them whether guilt was applicable to either, or to both, according to the evidence produced. The law, as laid down by the learned Attorney-General in the opening speech, had been acquiesced in by both of the learned counsel who appeared for the two prisoners; and he did not think it necessary, therefore, to say more than this—that what the Jury had to consider was, first, whether there had been such by his death by violence—whether, in other words, it was considered; secondly, whether either of the prisoners, or both, were participators in that violence?

whether they both were directly or immediately parties to the violence, or whether either of them committed the violence, with the knowledge and acquiescence, and acquiescence of the other. If they believed that they were both directly participators in the violence, then their verdict should be against both. As, also, if it was the violent act of either of them, with the previous consent and concurrence of the other, then they must bring in a verdict of "Guilty" against both. But if they believed that the act was known to one only, and that no previous consent was given by the other, then the verdict should be against that person. If they thought neither of them had to do with it, or if it should turn out that there were no means before them of casting the blame upon one more than the other, it was possible that they might acquit both. These were the points which the Jury were called upon to discover in this case, and he did not think it necessary further to occupy their attention with laying down any technical rules, or occupying their time by adverting to the counts in the indictment. The crime in question was, perhaps, one of the most unexampled ever recorded in the history of this country; but he did not mean to make any comments on its enormity. It was the duty of the Jury to enter upon the inquiry with as much calmness as possible, dismissing from their recollections everything they had heard before they entered the court, and to consider carefully everything founded on truth that could ultimately lead them to a just conclusion. The first question they had to consider was, had the crime been committed at all by anybody; and the next was, whether either of the prisoners, or one or both of them, were guilty of that crime. With respect to the first, it was admitted, on all hands, that Patrick O'Connor, the deceased, was murdered some time on Thursday, the 9th day of August; and his body was found in the state described by the surgeon, the skull having been perforated by a bullet, and the back of it fractured so as to present no fewer than 16 pieces of broken bone. If a body so circumstanced had been found anywhere, the conclusion that the person had been murdered would not, probably, have been irresistible. Had the body, however, been found buried, as it was, in the back kitchen, with wounds of an equivocal kind, leaving it ambiguous whether the individual had caused his own death, or whether death had been caused by murder, still, finding a body thus concealed and thus strangely buried from all human sight, in all probability they would have considered it as murdered, though the signs of violence left it doubtful whether his own hands or the hands of others inflicted the wounds; because some one must have been there to bury the body, and it would not have been placed in that condition unless some one had deprived the individual of life. When, therefore, they found the two circumstances united, viz. that the body was strangely concealed; and, when brought to light, presented a spectacle such as the surgeon had described—there could be no doubt whatever that a murder had been committed. Neither did there appear to be any doubt that Patrick O'Connor was murdered on the 9th of August. The question then arose, by whom was he murdered? The question then very naturally arose, who were the parties living in the house, in the back kitchen of which the body was found, and what was the history of those parties during the days that elapsed between the time when O'Connor was last seen and the time when his body was found on the 17th of August? The only two persons at that time living in the house were the prisoners at the bar. It had not been suggested by either of the learned counsel for the prisoners that the murder could have been committed by any other than the inmates of the house, nor had it been represented that anybody out of the house committed the murder, and brought the body and deposited it in the kitchen. There could be no doubt, then, that very grave suspicion must exist against the persons living in the house. The surgeon who examined the body was asked how long he thought it had been buried, and he replied, that it must have been buried about a week. That was on Friday, the 17th of August; and Thursday, the 9th of August, was the day on which the deceased disappeared. He had been seen at half-past seven that morning by the persons at whose house he lodged; he had been seen on London-bridge by more than one person at two different times; he had been seen, also, within 100 or 150 yards of the house of the prisoners some few minutes after five o'clock; but from that time he had not been seen, till his body was dug up in the back kitchen, on the 17th. The two prisoners at the bar appeared by different counsel, and they had attempted to throw the blame of this transaction, this dreadful crime, the one upon the other. One of the learned gentlemen directly and openly repudiated, on the part of the man, all share in the crime, and threw the guilt upon the woman; while the other learned gentleman, not quite so openly, but still distinctly enough, endeavoured to exculpate the woman, and throw the guilt upon the man. The Jury, however, must attend to the evidence, as well as to the observations of counsel, and, by their own experience and sound judgment, come to a conclusion as to where the guilt rested, and whether it belonged to the one or the other, or both. In taking a review of the whole transaction, it appeared to him that it would be very unsafe to rely upon small minute circumstances, as to which there might be no sure sources of information. They were to take a broad, general, comprehensive view of the case, not stopping to inquire, just at one particular moment, what would be the expressions of a man or, woman in the circumstances that might attach to that particular occasion; but to consider what was the result of all the circumstances brought out in the evidence laid before them. There were some things that it would well become them to consider with respect to the joint intentions of the two prisoners at the bar, and to these he would endeavour to call their attention when considering the prominent facts brought out in the evidence which they had heard in detail;

secondly, whether either of the prisoners in that violence

With respect to the male prisoner, he stated that he was present at the murder; that he saw his wife fire a pistol at the head of the deceased. Now this was conclusive evidence that he was present at that moment, and it was a natural inquiry whether he knew anything at it before. Was it a matter of which he had not the slightest anticipation, or was it one that he had reason to expect? It appeared that, when he gave an account of the transaction, to the sergeant of police, he said he was "anxious to go to town, as he wished to explain all." But had he explained anything? There was an allusion made to there being other wounds besides that produced by a shot, but he gave no explanation relative to them. He was told there were other wounds, but he gave no answer. Now, assuming that the male prisoner was present when somebody fired the pistol—he (the Chief Baron) used that expression because it was no evidence against the other prisoner—assuming that he was present when some person put one hand on the man's shoulder, and with the other hand fired the pistol, then the question came to be, who inflicted the wounds on the back of the head afterwards? What course did he here take? Did he endeavour to prevent any further violence? These were questions which the Jury must put to themselves, and endeavour to answer. As against the male prisoner, this seemed to be the case; he admitted he was present at the murder, but he gave no account of the rest of the transaction, or of the concealment of the body. It appeared that, after the murder, both the male and female prisoners quitted the house, and went off in different directions. Mrs. Manning, it appeared, went on Monday, the 13th of August; while the male prisoner left on the Wednesday morning following. [His Lordship then proceeded to direct the attention of the Jury to the other more prominent facts of the case, as brought out in evidence. In conclusion, he said:—] I believe that these are all the facts of the case on the part of the prosecution. No evidence has been called on the other side. It will be your duty to say to what conclusion your minds have been brought as to the participation in the murder by one or both of the prisoners. If you think that the one is guilty, and the other innocent, but cannot possibly decide which is the guilty party, you may be reduced to the alternative of returning a verdict of "Not guilty" as regards both. But, if you consider that one of them was guilty, it will be for you to consider whether, seeing that the murder was committed in the house where both the prisoners lived, it could possibly be undertaken by the one without the knowledge of the other. If you think it possible that, in the ordinary course of human nature, this could have happened, you will, of course, act upon your judgment ; but I trust your judgment will be well weighed before you pronounce it. If, indeed, you seriously believe that one of the parties alone has been guilty of the deed, and that the other had no private knowledge of the transaction, it will be for you to consider to which of the persons the guilt and innocence respectively applies. But if, looking at the whole transaction, you come to the conclusion that both must, according to the ordinary course of human affairs, have been concerned in the murder, then it will be your duty to find both prisoners guilty. With respect to any question of doubt—if, indeed, this be a case where any of the facts can be doubted—it will be for you to decide what part of the evidence you think true, and what you think objectionable. With respect to the doubts, I apprehend that your duty is calmly and gravely to investigate the case, to see what is the conclusion impressed upon your minds, as men of the world, as men of sense, and men of solid justice. If the conclusion to which you are conducted be that there is that degree of certainty in the case that you would act upon it in your own grave and important concerns, that is the degree of certainty which the law requires, and which will justify you in returning a verdict of guilty against one or both of the prisoners. It is not necessary that a crime should be established beyond the possibility of doubt. There are crimes committed in darkness and secrecy which can only be traced and brought to light by a comparison of circumstances, which press upon the mind more and more as they are increased in number. There are doubts more or less involved in every human transaction. We are frequently mistaken as to what we suppose we have seen—still oftener as to what we suppose we have heard. In all the transactions of life there is a certain degree of doubt mixed up, but these are not the doubts upon which you act in deciding upon a case so important as this for the public, on the one hand, and the prisoners on the other. I doubt not that you will discharge your duty most faithfully. You will consider that you have on the one hand a duty to the public —namely, to take care that the guilty shall not escape; and that, on the other, you have a duty to the prisoners—to take care that they shall not be convicted upon any mere surmise or suspicion—upon rash or light grounds, but upon grave and solid reasons presenting themselves to your understandings, and leading you to a satisfactory conclusion that one or both are guilty of the crime. With these remarks I dismiss you to the performance of your important duty, and I pray that your decision may be founded upon justice and truth.

The Jury retired exactly at six o'clock, and remained absent for three-quarters of an hour. During their absence the prisoners were allowed to retire, and the audience occupied themselves in eager conversation on the merits of the case and the probable verdict that would be returned. The dock, which was by this time nearly filled with spectators, was ordered to be cleared.

On the return of the Jury, at a quarter to seven o'clock, the prisoners were again placed at the bar. The loud buzz of conversation in the court at once gave way to solemn silence.

THE VERDICT.

Mr. Streight (Clerk of the Arraigns) said: Gentlemen of the Jury, do you find the prisoner Frederick George Manning Guilty or Not Guilty?

Foreman: GUILTY.

Mr. Streight: Do you find the prisoner Maria Manning Guilty or Not Guilty?

Foreman: GUILTY.

Mr. Streight: Frederick George Manning and Maria Manning, you severally stand convicted of the murder of Patrick O'Connor; what have you, or either of you, to say why the Court should not proceed to pass judgment upon you according to law?

MRS. MANNING'S ADDRESS TO THE COURT.

Mrs. Manning, in a state of great excitement, addressed the Court as follows. She spoke with a strong foreign accent, and with remarkable vehemence, her excitement appearing to supply her with fluency of speech:—There is no justice (she said) and no right for a foreign subject in this country. There is no law for me. I have had no protection—neither from the Judges, nor from the prosecutors, nor from my husband. I am unjustly condemned by this Court. If I were in my own country, I could prove that I had money sent from abroad, which is now in the Bank of England. My solicitors and counsel could have called witnesses to identify shares that were bought with my own money. Mr. O'Connor was more to me than my husband. He was a friend and brother to me ever since I came to this country. I knew him for seven years. He wanted to marry me, and I ought to have been married to him. I have letters which would prove his respect and regard for me ; and I think, considering that I am a woman and alone, that I have to fight against my husband's statements, that I have to fight against the prosecutors, and that even the Judge himself is against me—I think that I am not treated like a Christian, but like a wild beast of the forest; and the Judges and Jury will have it upon their consciences for giving a verdict against me. I am not guilty of the murder of Mr. O'Connor. If I had wished to commit murder, I would not have attempted the life of the only friend I had in the world—a man who would have made me his wife in a week, if I had been a widow. I have lived in respectable families, and can produce testimonials of character for probity in every respect, if inquiry is made. I can account for more money than was equal to the trifling shares that were found upon me. If my husband, through jealousy, and a revengeful feeling against O'Connor, chose to murder him, I don't see why I should be punished for it. I wish I could have expressed myself better in the English language. That is all I have to say.

Manning said nothing.

THE SENTENCE.

Mr. Justice Cresswell (who, in the absence of the Chief Baron, delivered judgment) then put on the black cap and addressed the prisoners as follows:—Frederick George Manning and Maria Manning, you have been convicted of the crime of murder——

Mrs. Manning (vehemently): No, no; I wont stand here to hear that said. You ought to be ashamed of yourselves. There is neither law nor justice here. [She then turned round as if to leave the dock, but was prevented by Mr. Cope, the Governor of Newgate, who stood behind her.]

Mr. Justice Cresswell: You have been defended by able counsel.

Mrs. Manning: They did not produce any witnesses for me.

Mr. Justice Cresswell: Every topic which ingenuity or experience had taught them would be at all available for your defence, has been urged by them. You have been found guilty by a Jury upon evidence which, I will venture to say, could leave no rational doubt upon the mind of any human being who heard it. A verdict of guilty is the only one which the Jury could conscientiously return. Had they failed to return that verdict, it would have been very difficult indeed to convince me that they had not shrunk from their duty, so completely was I satisfied, by the evidence which I heard detailed by the different witnesses, of the guilt of both of you.

Mrs. Manning: The witnesses in my favour were not called.

Mr. Justice Cresswell: Murder is the highest crime that one individual can commit against another in this country. It is at all times a horrible offence ; but the present murder was one of the most cold-blooded and deliberately calculated I ever remember to have heard or read of. Under the pretence of friendship, or rather affection—for such was the description of the invitation of the 8th—under that pretence, you unhappily deluded him to a place where his grave was probably then prepared, and where the deed was afterwards committed which had, no doubt, been for days contemplated. It is one of the most appalling instances of human wickedness which the annals of this court can furnish. It has been suggested that the deceased led a vicious course of life with one of you prisoners; but whether that was so or not, I profess not to judge; that rests with your own conscience. But, whatever was his course of life, without a moment's warning of the preparation, without the slightest opportunity of thinking of futurity, or endeavouring to seek pardon for any offences he had committed, that unhappy man was hurried into eternity. The law, more merciful, allows to you space of time for preparation. It appears that, on a former occasion, a conversation passed between one of you and the witness Massey as to where the soul of a person who had committed a murder would go. The time has arrived when you should ask that question again. As I cannot hold out the slightest hope of a commutation of the sentence which I am about to pronounce, I am bound to tell you that, as far as my judgment goes, your doom is irretrievably fixed when that sentence is passed. I advise you, therefore, to resort, with all humility, and all contrition, to the advice and counsel of the minister of the Gospel appointed to attend you. From him you will receive all the consolation which, in your unhappy condition, he can, in the faithful discharge of his duties, afford you. From him you will learn what you have to fear. He will no doubt point out to you, in strong terms, the full extent of your guilt; and I am sure he will rejoice if he can conscientiously hold out to you any hope of that pardon hereafter which, in this world, is impossible. I consign you to his advice, and pray you to profit by it. Whatever sorrow, or even indignation, you may really feel, or affect to feel, as to the course of proceeding this day, depend upon it that others will judge differently; and I doubt whether every one who has heard the trial will not be as well satisfied as I am that the result is the only one consistent with justice. Having given you this warning and advice, which I pray you once more to receive in all humility, it remains for me only to pronounce the dread sentence of the law, which is, that you be taken hence to her Majesty's gaol for the county of Surrey, and thence to the place of execution, and there be severally hanged by the neck until you be dead; and that afterwards your dead bodies be buried within the precincts of the gaol in which you shall be confined after this sentence; and may the Lord have mercy upon your guilty souls!

Mr. Streight: Amen.

Mrs. Manning was again proceeding to address the Court, when she was ordered to be removed. She exclaimed that it was shameful to pass such a sentence upon her, and added, "Base and shameful England!" According to custom, the bench in front of the dock was strewn with rue. Taking some of this in her hand, she threw it into the body of the court, as if by that contemptuous act she could find some relief from the excitement under which she laboured. She was immediately removed by Mr. Cope and a female turnkey.

Manning merely bowed to the Court and retired. He seemed very subdued, but retained his self-possession.

The proceedings closed shortly after seven o'clock.

The following letter, which led to the renewal of the intimacy between the prisoner Maria Manning and the unfortunate deceased, will doubtless be perused with interest by the public. It proceeded as follows:—

"Customs, St. Katherine's Docks, June 11th, 1847.

"My dear Mrs. ——,—Not knowing your real name, I have addressed this note as usual. I hope it will find you. I cannot describe to you my feelings, and what I suffered since I saw you last evening. If you were to know half you would have compassion for me, if I was the greatest enemy you ever had. I have spent a solitary and dreary winter and a dull and melancholy spring, in anticipation of having a jovial and pleasant autumn. I had given up going into all society—cut the acquaintance of every friend I had on your account, being anxious to economise and secure for ourselves the means of making us happy and comfortable the rest of our lives. I had my month's leave of absence settled to commence on the 6th of August, when I thought you might be after returning from the Continent, and intended to get married on the 7th, leave London for Boulogne on the 8th, and there spend the honey-month; but, alas! these arrangements are now blighted. You have all these comforts that your heart can wish for, and I am glad of it. For poor me there is none of these consolations left, but the sad reflection of being disappointed. Ah, Maria! You have acted cruel to me. Why not, like a true professor of what you avowed, write and say what you intended before you acted so—then, at the risk of losing my situation, I would go every step to Erskine House and get married to the only being on the face of God's earth who could make me happy; and, Maria dear, if you could only read the feelings of my heart you would not do as you did. However, it is too late to be speaking of these things now. We must be reconciled with the will of God, and hope all things are regulated by Him for a wise and benevolent purpose. Enough now of this sad and melancholy affair, for so it is to me. However, I hope we will always entertain the same kindly feelings towards each other that is due to old friends. I can speak for myself, and am sure I will. When shall I have the pleasure of seeing you here? Bring your husband, and any others you like; I will be able to show them the docks, and the vaults; but, mind, ladies are not admitted into the vaults after one o'clock; I wish you could come soon. There is a ship from China, alongside my station in the docks—the *Viscount Sandon*; she leaves on Sunday. There are three Chinese on board, and it would be a novelty for you to see them with their long tails. You said you would call on me on Sunday. I wish you would. If you do, write and say what time, that I may be sure to meet you. You may be able to give some explanations on the matter, which may smooth it down a little. I wish I could acquit you of infidelity on the occasion. I hope that the blessing of God may rest on all your proceedings, and believe me, under any circumstances, till death,—Yours very affectionately, PATRICK O'CONNOR."

London: W. M. CLARK, Warwick-lane, Paternoster-row.

THE BERMONDSEY MURDER.

COURT OF EXCHEQUER CHAMBER.—(THIS DAY.)
THE CASE OF MRS. MANNING.

This being the day appointed for the hearing of the arguments in favour of Mrs. Manning being tried by a jury *de medietate linguæ*, the Court was crowded from an early hour with a large number of barristers and other gentlemen.

Six of the learned Judges entered and took their seats on the bench shortly after 10 o'clock. They consisted of the Chief Justice (Wilde), the Chief Baron (Pollock), Mr. Baron Rolfe, Mr. Justice Coleridge, Mr. Baron Platt, and Mr. Justice Cresswell.

Mr. Ballantine (with whom was Mr. Parry) appeared for Mrs. Manning; Mr. Saunders appeared for Mr. Manning; the Attorney-General appeared on behalf of the Crown.

MR. BALLANTINE argued the question at very considerable length, citing the various statutes, and commenting upon them as he proceeded, concluding by urging upon the Court that the female prisoner was legally entitled to have a new trial by a foreign jury *de medietate linguæ*.

The ATTORNEY-GENERAL replied, contending that the prisoner was a naturalized subject, and that therefore she had been fairly tried, and was not entitled to the privilege claimed for her.

The Judges retired at 1 o'clock to consult, and upon their return into Court,

The Lord CHIEF JUSTICE said, that the Judges were unanimously of opinion that the objection, urged at the trial on the part of the prisoner, could not be sustained. The only question which they had to decide was, whether or not at the time of the trial the prisoner was an alien. If she was, she was entitled to the privilege she claimed, but if she was a naturalized subject she was not so entitled. The Court were of opinion, and all the great text-writers laid down the doctrine, that a foreign female marrying a British-born subject became naturalized, and as the prisoner was at the time of the trial so married, the Judges were unanimously of opinion that she was not entitled to the privilege she claimed, and, therefore, they dismissed the appeal.

Milton Keynes UK
Ingram Content Group UK Ltd.
UKHW022315230823
427327UK00005B/88